MW00764148

The Exquisite Zodiac

Why the Signs Are the Way They Are and What it Means for You

RICK DICLEMENTE

WITH LIZA JANE BROWN

The Exquisite Zodiac:

Why the Signs Are the Way They Are and What it Means for You

Copyright © 2011

By Rick DiClemente with Liza Jane Brown

All rights reserved. Reproduction or translation of any part of this book through any means without permission of the copyright owner is unlawful, except for promotional use. Request for other permissions or further information should be addressed in writing to the publisher.

ISBN-13: 978-1467986816

Cover Design, Interior Layout and Illustrations: Kathy Then

Editor: Gina Mazza

Rick DiClemente
1002 Greentree Road, Suite 107
Pittsburgh, PA 15220

1   0   9   8   7   6   5   4

Table of Contents

Acknowledgements

I would like to acknowledge the late Kay Lucas, who helped me get started in this baffling world of astrology many years ago. I will forever be indebted to Ann Riesbeck DiClemente, who stuck by my side for many years with encouragement and belief in my abilities. I have special appreciation for Jamie Stiles and Susan Rose for helping me so much in my early days.

A special thank you goes out to Gladys Edmunds for her professional guidance; Gina Mazza for her initial faith in me, as well as her editorial prowess and wise advice; and to Kathy Then for her creative artwork and layout.

Thank you to my mother, who was such a brave, giving soul, and to my father, who taught me about the power of silence.

But mostly, I would like to express my thanks to my partner, Liza Jane Brown, who has been my steady hand throughout this entire process. Without her, this book would never have been written.

Dedication

This book is dedicated to my ever-nascent son, Taylor

Introduction

It's the most vivid experience I've ever had yet much of this same memory remains blurred to this day. I was in a bookstore in 1978 when *The Compleat Astrologer* by Derek and Julia Parker jumped off of the shelf and landed in my hands. Did it actually jump, or was I so mesmerized by this particular book that it only felt that way? (That's the part that remains hazy.) Either way, this experience was accompanied by a message that came through my intuition with such clarity that it was shocking and stunning at the same time: *"This is what you are supposed to do."*

It was an undeniable *knowing*, and I was so appreciative to have been unexpectedly given such clear grace. From that moment on, there was *no doubt about it.* Wow. Imagine that: knowing what I'm supposed to do. Now all I had to do was learn *how* to do it. Fortunately, that part came easy for me. Inexplicably, I had a natural affinity for the topic.

Several decades and thousands of astrology charts later, I remain mind-blown by my adventure into the intricacies of astrology. The thing that is *most* incomprehensible to me is that this fascinating art and science remains such a mystery to most of mankind. It's such a useful tool for explaining so much of our lives that it only makes common sense to use it. Astrology's truth is there, just waiting to be revealed and scrutinized by trained eyes—and, by the way, you don't have to be *that* trained to begin to see it (although it does take years before one is ready to read for other people).

Part of the problem is that people have a misconception about what astrology is and can do. I have had the good fortune of speaking to small and large groups on this, my favorite subject, and almost everywhere I go, people want to hear astrology explained in terms that they can understand.

Many followers of astrology are labeled as unrealistic or escapist. It's not that they want to escape reality, as many incorrectly think. They are simply reaching for understanding of what makes them tick. Many people just can't see how astrology works and won't give it any consideration. Let me say this up front: I completely understand anyone who doesn't believe in this subject. After all, why should you believe in it, unless you've studied it? Until its validity has been proven to you by a reputable astrologer, the value of this science would probably slip under the radar of your daily focus.

Fortunately, however, there are many folks out there who intuit that astrology simply works, that there is something to it. Hardly anyone knows how; it just does. Explaining how astrology works is extremely complicated. "As above, so below" is the best explanation I can give you. The universal force that is at the source of your being is one and the same as the clockwork energies that move the planets and all things. All things are connected and in sync. Basically, all an astrologer does is read the clock hands—that is, the planetary positions. Both planets and people have the same basic harmonic rhythms. This is a topic far beyond the scope of this book but is important to at least mention.

Nearly everybody wants to hear about themselves. Most of us are closely melded to our own "story." Too many times, we're downright obsessed with our "his-story" or "her-story," way too closely for our own balanced well being. Astrology helps us to get more detached from our own melodrama because we start to see the common threads and patterns of behavior that we all share, such as jealousy, pride, emotional need, and so forth. These patterns of energy (or, archetypes) parallel perfectly with the natures of the signs of the zodiac.

In large part, I stopped reading astrology books about 20 years ago. My path led me away from how other astrologers see things. It's not that they're wrong, it's just that I wanted to learn directly in an unfiltered way by watching people's reactions to life. I chose instead to observe people and watch the planets, signs and energies in motion in everyday situations. When we say, for example, "What got into him?" or "Something's come over her," that's exactly what I'm talking about. Those *are* the planetary energies moving through the signs. Even though the heart of this book is not about the planets, we really can't talk about astrology without somehow blending the signs and planets; they are too interrelated. Both planets and signs have their own archetypal patterns, and we will discuss how the planets "influence" the signs in one of the final chapters.

Astrologers know what those energies are, how they are likely to be experienced, and when the experience of those energies will likely peak and fade. While we think of the planets and stars as far up in the cosmos, these energies are not "out there"; they are inside of us. Tracking these archetypal energies, as well as my overall fever for astrology, hasn't stopped since 1978.

The Astrological Zodiac is Life's Prism

What I have discovered by reading natal charts and going through miles of confusing mental mazes, or individualized charts, is that the zodiac is a phenomenal tool. Its truth displays itself as vividly as a prism yields its spectrum of brilliant colors. The twelve signs of the zodiac are a family of unified yet extremely varied energy panoramas; however, I have found that most astrology books are lacking when it comes to explaining why the signs are the way they are.

Most astrological explanations have told us *how* and *what* the signs are. You've heard it all before: Taureans are stubborn, Aquarians are offbeat and Geminis are two people. The older astrology books seem to represent a god that was simply in twelve different moods when He/She/It invented or coined the twelve zodiacal signs.

The Exquisite Zodiac goes deeper. What do the Libra scales really mean? *Why* is Capricorn so different from its preceding sign of Sagittarius? Just *why* is the sign of Cancer so moody when it's right next to the sign of Leo, which seems emotionally rock solid? *Why* is the first sign of the zodiac, Aries, so "self-oriented," when the final sign of Pisces is so much the opposite?

After decades of studying these very questions and many others, comparing signs, digging for the truths, reading charts for people, watching world events and more, I believe that this book presents a pretty complete picture of what lies at the heart of each sign, its archetypal imprint, as well as an exposé of how each sign of the zodiac is largely birthed from its completion of the sign preceding it.

A sign is a sign. If the Sun was in that sign at the time of your birth, then that is your Sun sign. If the Moon was in that sign at the time of your birth, then that is your Moon sign.

Even though we all have many different influences from several signs in our natal charts, the main message here is that the descriptions in this book concentrate on the pure essence of each of the twelve main sign archetypes. If we were discussing the color spectrum, this work would define the reds, yellows and blues: the primary colors. We have to define each color before we can even think of combining different hues.

The Exquisite Zodiac exposes the truth lying deep at the heart of the mysterious dozen. Bear with me through these chapters, try to broaden the lens through which you view astrology and I sincerely believe that you will find this information to be enlightening and life changing. Before you can tackle this complex subject, you have to have an objective, unbiased perspective of the basis of astrology: the twelve signs.

For starters, we're going to need to understand some preliminary principles before we can auger deeper into the subject. Hundreds of astrology books cover these basics but assuming you haven't read anything on this topic yet, I'll quickly present some fundamental concepts. Then we will delve into fathoming the kernels of the obscured meanings of each sign's archetype—or, natural pattern, if you will.

Deep within each sign's imprint lies a force field that drives us: its archetype. It is alive, vibrant, intelligent and its essential nature is integral to the whole. By heeding its call, we not only stay in sync with ourselves but also with the universe. The time has come for us to comprehend our deeper connection to our own individual archetypal patterns, as well our connection to the larger collective.

Once you understand the zodiac's archetypal basis, you are well on your way to understanding how astrology works. Astrology is a complex subject;

no wonder few people can interpret birth charts, let alone put up with its sometimes maddening idiosyncrasies and seeming inconsistencies. Yet, when you have demonstrated that you have had the patience to tame this rich lady, you'll find that her jewels really do provide a special kind of dowry—the precious gift of self-understanding.

— *Rick DiClemente*
September 2011

....

We all yearn for insight and guidance as we travel along life's rocky path towards fulfilling our dreams and aspirations. So, it's no wonder that we fall prey to believing the pronouncements found in "daily horoscope" columns. We come seeking clarity on matters of importance to us but here's the rub: the generalized predictions and innuendo often found in newspaper astrology columns, online blogs and mass market astrology books only serve to tantalize and further confound us. It's easy to get frustrated trying to make sense out of "star guides" that seem *kind* of true, at best.

What we read in these ambiguous sources usually is only partly true because astrology that is based solely on Sun signs can barely scratch the surface of this often misunderstood and misrepresented, yet truly vast and profound discipline called astrology. Even if few of us have the time and passion to endlessly mine the depths of astrology's riches, we can *all* benefit in innumerable ways from learning just a little bit about it.

When Rick and I began talking about this book and why we wanted to write it, I first thought of Mike, an astrology student of Rick's who we saw at a dinner party several years ago. Mike shared an observation with us: "Once I began to see how each of us experience life according to the astrological archetypes we embody," he noted, "I became much more understanding and forgiving of *everybody*, including myself." As Mike's revelation illustrates, astrology can have a deep and far-reaching impact on the quality of one's life.

Our purpose in writing this book, therefore, is to share astrological insights that are easy to understand and apply in daily life. Based on our experiences with clients and students, we are confident that you will come away from this book with a greater equanimity and increased understanding of yourself, others and the world at large.

We also hope to convey in these chapters the multidimensional, holographic qualities of the zodiacal archetypes, which offer a glimpse into the depth and potential that exists within not only ourselves but the cosmos.

As we find ourselves on the cusp of the Age of Aquarius, humanity is increasingly able to intuit that every life on earth is connected to all others in ways that most of us have not previously understood, and that our individual and collective well being, and the evolution of personal and group consciousness are, therefore, intertwined. God is not only "out there"; *each* of us is part of the fabric of divine intelligence. As we continue to realize our divine intelligence, we can also recognize our responsibility to use it wisely and collaboratively for our mutual uplifting. All manner of previously considered esoteric knowledge, including astrology, must be and is being made accessible to anyone who welcomes it as a tool to help meet the challenges and embrace the opportunities that this age affords.

Rick and I would be very happy if this book contributes in some meaningful way to the fulfillment of your potential and to the highest manifestation of the Aquarian age.

Wishing peace and love to all,
— Liza Jane Brown

How to Use this Book

You are probably already somewhat acquainted with Sun sign basics; if so, much of the content of this book will sound familiar. This familiarity can give you the benefit of a place to hang your hat but in order to get as much out of this book as possible, *it is very important to remember that each of our birth charts embody many aspects of different signs that include, but are not limited to, what we know as our Sun sign.*

The facets and layered meaning of each of the twelve archetypes of the zodiac apply to all twelve "planets," all twelve "houses" of the chart and other important factors—all of which comprise an individual's natal chart. In this way, your chart symbolizes the complex being that we really are; your essence cannot be contained by your Sun sign alone!

For example, at the time of your birth, the Sun may have been in the sign of Gemini but you feel as though you don't fit much of what you read about the sign of Gemini. If Scorpio was on the horizon (your "rising sign",) if the Moon was in the sign of Libra and four planets were in the sign of Leo when you were born, you are likely to feel as much, if not more, like these other signs than Gemini. This is because you also strongly embody these other zodiacal archetypes. Most of us have four, five or even six major zodiacal themes in our natal charts, and the possible permutations are countless.

Therefore, when reading this book it is best to keep in mind the following:

1. If you are tempted to dive right into the chapter that discusses your Sun sign, go ahead but keep in mind that each of us is influenced to varying degrees by *all* the archetypes of the zodiac. For this reason, we encourage you to read the entire book from front to back. As you read, you will probably discover several zodiacal archetypes, in addition to your Sun sign, that also seem to describe who you are.

2. We define "archetype" as Richard Tarnas does in *An Introduction to Archetypal Astrological Analysis*: "A universal principle or force that affects—impels, structures, permeates—the human psyche and human behaviors on many levels…" We use terms such as "pattern" and "paradigm" interchangeably with "archetype."

3. Be aware that each sign of the zodiac's archetype has internal consistency and is multi-faceted at the same time. You may express some qualities of a certain archetype and not express others at all. For example, a particular Virgo may not be the neatest person but still expresses perfectionistic tendencies at their job. At first, you may not see how different manifestations of the same archetype share the same principles but the more you study and observe, the more you will develop a feel for this.

4. Keep in mind that the "planets" referred to in this book include Sun, Moon, Mercury, Venus, Earth, Mars, Jupiter, Saturn, Chiron, Uranus, Neptune and Pluto. While some of these are not considered planets to astronomers, they all serve the essential, archetypal functions of planets in an astrological sense.

5. The use of inclusive terms such as "mankind" or "Cosmic Man" within this text is a concession to the lack of appropriate gender-neutral terms in the English language. Their use is not meant to devalue the feminine/female principle or aspect of humankind.

6. We use terms such as "soul," "spirit" and "Self" more broadly than they may be used within the context of specific religious doctrines.

7. We present these astrological insights not to confine you to narrow concepts of your archetypes but to expand your conception of who you are and who you might become. The astrology that we know and practice can be a means to empower you, not limit your free will.

Times have never been better to learn about astrology. In addition to many fine astrology books that are available in print, the Internet makes it easy to calculate your personal chart and study online; e-books, newsletters, discussion groups, online courses and the services of astrologers are all available at the click of mouse. We encourage you to find and consult with competent astrologers, especially face to face, when you can. There is no substitute for dialogue with an excellent astrologer who can help you recognize and work with your archetypal energies more intentionally toward your greater consciousness and fulfillment.

Mining For The Diamond In The Rough:
An Overview of the Zodiac's Six Archetypal Variants

At a level just below our consciousness lies a very little known world of archetypal energies. This is the level where astrology is operative. We can sense these important rumblings but don't always know what to "do" with them. These universal archetypal urges are but one of our connections to the larger cosmos and its omniscience. This book attempts to map out and clearly explain six of the main variants that "cause" each of the signs of the zodiac to have their individuated nature.

These promptings are not easy to understand as they are not specific and in fact are always in a state of flux themselves. We live in a complex, ever-evolving world. By understanding and staying in tune with these archetypal imperatives, we improve our chances of being in synchronization with our inner world as well as our "outer" one.

It's no wonder that astrology is so confusing! Astrologers calibrate and gauge one zodiacal wheel full of *planets*, spinning on top of another circle of *signs*, and yet another wheel of *houses*. Add to the mix that these planets, signs and houses are all moving in different directions at different speeds simultaneously. It can be downright dizzying!

Yet if you are patient and take the time to study this accurate and marvelously intimate science, you can discern early on how highly individualized and meaningful the possible permutations in each person's archetypal template can be. Each tiny astrological stone contributes greater definition to the overall mosaic of your personal astrological birth chart.

As stated in the Introduction, mainstream acceptance of astrology has two great obstacles: 1) Many people completely identify with their Sun sign and often don't even know what that means, and 2) readers of daily "horoscopes" of questionable origin and validity think, *That's it, that's astrology.* Well, that's *not* it.

Let's start with subject one: the twelve signs—yes, the Sun signs *but not as you might know them.* Each sign has its own unique motif and nature. As I will say many times on these pages, if you truly understand *why* the signs are the way they are, then you will naturally understand *what* they are like. It is first important to notice that the characteristics assigned to these twelve ancient archetypes were not chosen willy-nilly. Their basic and rudimentary essences have been revealed to us over time as "known truth" and represent the core nature of life itself. In ancient times (and even today), consistent exposure to the night sky informed earth's natives of the universe's intelligent order.

Each of the twelve archetypes is very different from one another and there are many reasons why each sign is as it is. You see, I want you to understand why Aquarians are friendly but often tend to be aloof, or *why* a Libra is classy and oftentimes indecisive. You will see why all twelve of the signs are dissimilar, as well as alike.

After more than three decades of research, I have narrowed down the following comparative categories to six specific areas, what I will call six "archetypal variants" that explain why the signs differ from each other. Each will be described very briefly here then individually expounded upon in later chapters. At first, our discussion will be about the main factors that separate and define each sign. Then we'll go into greater detail about what makes each sign like it is. Finally, we'll address a detailed comparison of those six archetypal variants criteria across the span of each sign of the zodiac.

When we examine why each sign is what it is, we'll find it revealing to look at these six "archetypal variants." I will present both time-tested and novel principles to you in an overarching way in order to spread more light on this entire topic of *The Exquisite Zodiac.*

So let's begin our brief introduction of the six archetypal variants:

1. The twelve **stages of man**.

2. Each sign is **outgrowth** of the sign before it.

3. The three **modes** and four **elements.**

4. **Self-oriented** versus **other-oriented** signs.

5. Six **polarities** of signs.

6. **Ruling planets** of each sign.

The Twelve Stages of Man

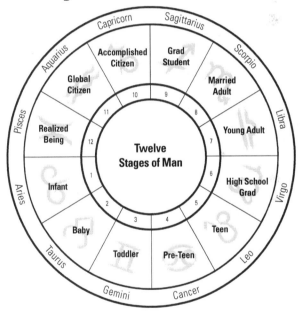

The twelve stages of development differentiate the basic nature deep within each sign. The names I have chosen for each stage are not absolute but they most closely parallel what actually takes place during each stage of life. Bear in mind that no rigid boundaries exist between each stage; rather, one blends into the next. Layers of other signs' archetypes are usually piled on top of other rudimentary archetypes, but it's the primary stage that provides the basic building block.

So, here is an explanation of the twelve stages of development as they relate to each of the twelve main signs.

Aries, the first sign of the zodiac, represents the stage of the *infant*. This does not mean that this archetype is infantile; it simply means that the essential nature is pure, innocent, direct and basically unassuming. This is their primary essence. Even so, the shadow side of the Aries archetype can exhibit childlike behavior; it all depends upon other facets in the personal horoscope, as well as many other factors. (As you will see, all signs have a shadow side.)

The key idea here is how the stage of Man seems.

Let me explain further. Each archetype has a "veneer," or outer sense. Just being around people of different signs gives us a sense of this childlike or elder-like feel. Some people seem playful, while others seem more sober.

The second "born," Taurus, is representative of the *baby* who starts to recognize what it has both in its physical environment, and as part of its natural persona. Gemini is indicative of the toddler, wandering in search of its new toys. And on and on we go, around the circle of the symbolic Man who becomes evermore complex.

> *This does not imply that you are born first as an Aries, then reincarnate as a Taurus, and so on. Again, these twelve stages of Man do not represent a sign's or person's level of maturity, or the state of evolution of that particular soul.*

Some of the most intelligent minds and influential human beings have been born to the signs of Aries and Taurus. Likewise, more than a few Aquarians and Pisces have plenty to learn about personal development. Many more detailed explanations of these twelve stages will be presented in upcoming chapters.

Each Sign Is an Outgrowth of the Sign Before It

This second archetypal variant may, in fact, be the most important aspect of the zodiac.

When examined closely, it becomes evident that each sign has a strong need to transcend the nature of the sign before it. They have "been there, done that." Taurus needs to calm down and anchor what Aries achieved. Scorpio needs to intensify and add depth to the relationship recently born in Libra. It is apparent how Capricorn has to pay the dues for the frivolousness of Sagittarius, and so on. As each sign manifests, develops and grows, there comes a time when it will cease *to exist if it persists in acting as it has.* Therefore it evolves to the next level; thus, the ensuing sign.

This keeps the zodiac fresh, alive and … exquisite.

Aries	~erupts boldly and is born into existence out of the Oneness/No-thing-ness of Pisces.
Taurus	~contains the fiery outburst of Aries, gets anchored, grounded and planted in order to foster.
Gemini's	~establishment of its roots is now complete, and now the limbs need to branch out and explore.
Cancer	~needs to slow down and nestle; now it is time to be nurtured in the waters of emotion.
Leo	~needs to overcome hypersensitivity, strengthen the self and gain confidence via extroversion.
Virgo	~refines the self, takes responsibility and becomes realistic about its self-definition (or, ego).
Libra	~via partnering socializes and establishes further identity by comparison to social norms.
Scorpio	~needs to go deeper into relationships; true marriage, devotion and loyalty to their partner.
Sagittarius	~needs to surpass one-on-one relationships and expand into the world in all ways.
Capricorn	~needs to take a social position and establish duty and responsibility to community.
Aquarius	~needs to recover individuality, and champion equality and brotherhood.
Pisces	~needs to transcend self-hood and vanish, only to become full once again in the Oneness of all things.

The Three Modes and Four Elements

Modes

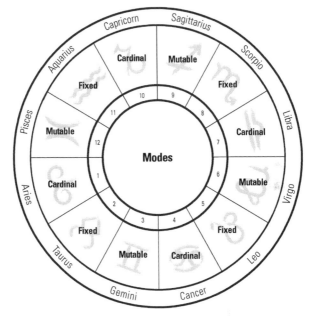

The mode of a sign represents the fundamental essence at the base of each sign. Astrology's **modes** are also known as "quadruplicities," or **cardinal, fixed** and **mutable**. (There are four of each one, totaling twelve.) Each mode forms a cross on the zodiac.

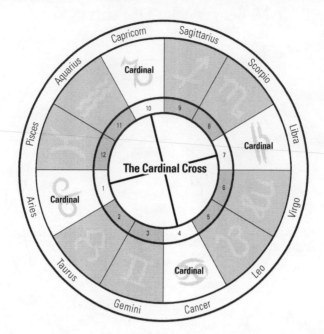

The four **cardinal** signs of Aries, Cancer, Libra and Capricorn are displayed in what is known as the cardinal cross. Members of the cardinal mode by definition are *leaders and generators*. They get things started.

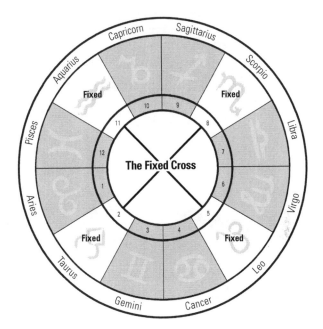

The second mode consisting of the signs of Taurus, Leo, Scorpio and Aquarius fall into the category known as the **fixed** cross. These signs naturally give strong emphasis to the rudimentary nature of their sign; namely they *add focus*, steadfastness, organizational skills and concentration.

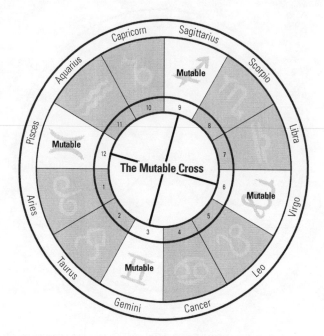

The final mode is known as **mutable**. The mutable cross consists of Gemini, Virgo, Sagittarius and Pisces. These signs are usually very flexible and have a strong need to disperse or give and exchange what they have.

Cardinal signs generate, fixed signs concentrate and mutable signs disperse.

No matter what modality your Sun sign belongs to, most charts have varying degrees of cardinal, fixed and mutable energies. As you can see, these three categories are very basic and give rise to fundamental archetypal construct of the personality. It must be emphasized that each of us is a complex, unique combination of these universal forces. We will revisit these three modes later as we unveil each sign and explore these criteria in detail.

Elements

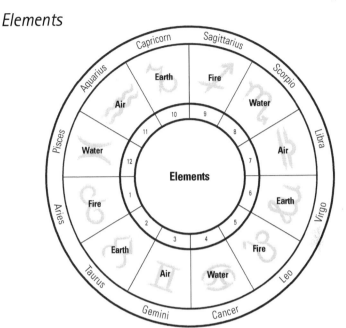

Now we address the other base energies of the zodiac known as the four **elements**. Fire, earth, air and water are another way of subdividing the twelve signs. (There are three of each element, totaling twelve.) They form the shape of a triangle on the zodiac. The elements describe how the mode is utilized or expressed in each particular sign.

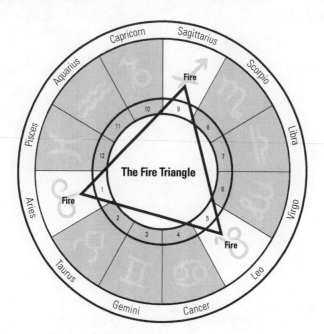

The **fire** signs of Aries, Leo and Sagittarius are filled with spirit, energy and a zest for life. They hunger for activity and their nature is to act without hesitation.

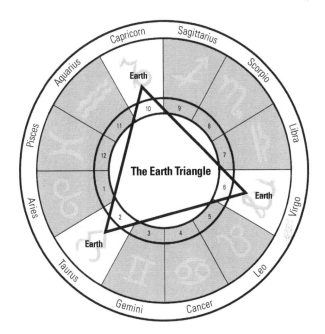

The second element is comprised of three **earth** signs: Taurus, Virgo and Capricorn. Earth signs are practical. As one would expect, earth signs are down to earth!

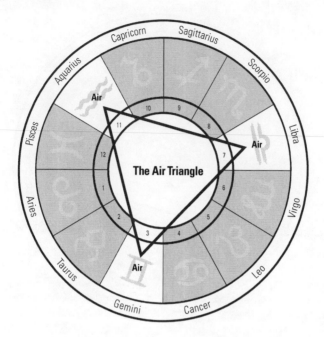

Air signs come next. The signs of Gemini, Libra and Aquarius represent our thinkers and communicators. Air is the element of the intellect and the exchange of ideas.

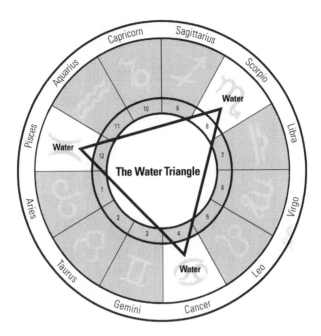

The final element is categorized as **water**, which represents feeling or emotion. Water may be the most important of the four. After all, *without love, all things become meaningless.* Cancer, Scorpio and Pisces, all members of the water element, naturally focus on feelings and all dimensions of love.

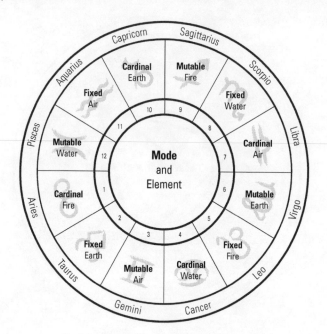

When we combine the three modes with the four elements, we end up with twelve distinct combinations. These provide us with an understanding of each sign's basic uniqueness. Aries is cardinal fire, Taurus is fixed earth, Gemini is mutable air, and so on. Because astrology is based upon the 3 modes and 4 elements is why we have twelve, and <u>only</u> twelve signs.

Self-Oriented versus Other-Oriented Signs

The first six signs of the zodiac represent the "Me" half of the zodiac; the last six signs; the "We" half. This orientation is indispensable in understanding the zodiac as a whole and is much overlooked in the overall purview of astrology.

Self-Oriented Signs

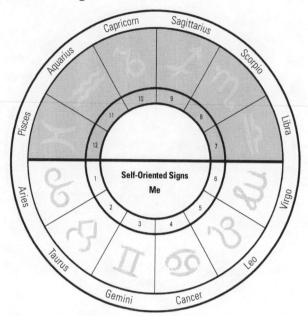

The six signs of the first half of the zodiac are *self-oriented*. This does not mean that individuals in this group are selfish, arrogant or self-absorbed, that they don't think about others. It does mean, however, that at *the archetypal level*, each of these signs has a need to define, develop, express and be quite attentive to the self. It is their main orientation.

Self-oriented = they get spirit, identification, confidence and learn from the self. This bears repetition: No sign is better, more advanced or more evolved than another.

Other-Oriented Signs

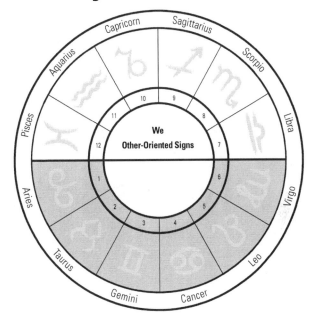

The final half-dozen signs are not only more inclined to be extra concerned with others, their very development and essential needs are based upon their interaction with them.

Other-oriented = they get spirit, identification, confidence and learn from the self via the interplay with others.

Six Polarities of Signs

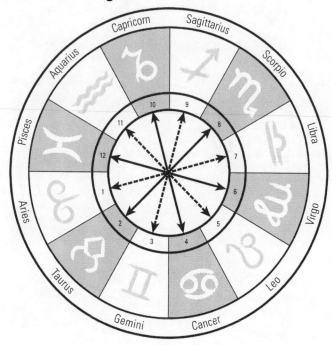

The zodiac has six pairs of signs. Every sign is very much like, yet different from, its opposite sign. They operate in a similar fashion yet in a *different field of reference*. For example, Aries, the first sign, is very focused on its own identity operating within the "self-oriented" half of the zodiac. Meanwhile, its opposing sign, Libra, is also focused on identity but operates in the "other-oriented" half. Therefore it finds its identity through engagement with its partnerships.

The other five polarities that we will cover in detail function in a similar way and are critical to understanding the zodiac and all of the signs.

Ruling Planets of Each Sign

A ruling planet lends much of its "feel" to the sign that it governs. Since this is not a book about the planets, I have minimized references to such; however, the upcoming chapters that detail each sign discuss each one's ruling planet and its effects. The differences between the sign's archetype and the ruling planet's archetype are not large yet are somewhat distinct. This can be confusing but for now, it is only necessary to understand that the two are very closely aligned.

In older classical astrology, there were seven planets ruling the twelve signs because at that time, only seven were known. This meant that five planets—Mercury, Venus, Mars, Jupiter and Saturn—had to share double duty. Then, during the past few hundred years, three other planets were discovered: Uranus, Neptune and Pluto. For a while, that meant that only Mercury and Venus had double-domains.

As of late it has become my firm opinion that we actually have twelve astrological "planets" matched one-on-one to the twelve signs. I agree with many current astrologers who think that newcomer Chiron is the sole ruler of Virgo. I propose that the Earth itself take on a new assignment of ruling Taurus. Each ruling planet will be presented with its associated sign in the chapters ahead and are listed in the diagrams above and below.

Signs	Traditional Rulers	Current Rulers	Suggested Rulers
Aries	Mars	Mars	Mars
Taurus	Venus	Venus	Earth**
Gemini	Mercury	Mercury	Mercury
Cancer	Moon	Moon	Moon
Leo	Sun	Sun	Sun
Virgo	Mercury	Mercury	Chiron**
Libra	Venus	Venus	Venus
Scorpio	Mars	Pluto*	Pluto
Sagittarius	Jupiter	Jupiter	Jupiter
Capricorn	Saturn	Saturn	Saturn
Aquarius	Saturn	Uranus*	Uranus
Pisces	Jupiter	Neptune*	Neptune

*new last 200 years   ** new since 1977

Part Two:

Cutting The Gem Into Twelve Perfect Facets: The Archetypes of the Zodiac's Twelve Signs

Aries: A Tremor in the Air

And the spirit of God moved upon the face of the waters…

During a past-life regression, I found myself seated at the top of a powerful waterfall. The facilitator asked if I was ready to take the

> *plunge into another lifetime, and I hesitantly said, "Well, okay!"*
> *Instantly, I felt the great plummeting flood of the waterfall and*
> *SWOOP! There I was, upside-down in utero! Cushiony. Dark.*
> *Serene. Silent…*

Out of the void comes the urge to be, the longing for existence—thus, Aries, the first sign of the zodiac. Individuals who are blessed with this daring impulse are fiery, adventurous and enthusiastic about life. This Arian archetype cannot be stopped or even stalled.

The virginal vastness of the Arian landscape emanates from the sea of the undifferentiated void that was once Pisces. The cosmic function of Aries is to *sprout into being.* The Bible's Genesis, "Out of the nothingness is born all things," captures this principle perfectly:

> *In the beginning God created the heaven and the earth.*
> *And the earth was without form, and void;*
> *and darkness was upon the face of the deep.*
> *And the Spirit of God moved upon the face of the waters.*
> *And God said, "Let there be light" and there was light.*

New Thought references to "manifestation" directly born out of "intention" are the very bases of many popular books, such as *The Secret* by Rhonda Bryne and *The Power of Intention* by Dr. Wayne Dyer, among others. Ancient wisdom speaks of this, as well. Within The Buddha's stillness lies the unmanifest; the lotus bursting forth is the "Aries," the act of becoming—*is-ness*—the great I AM.

This same concept has been expounded upon by many writers over the millennia. Author Carlos Castaneda referred to the "nagual" (the sea of nothingness, or the unmanifest) becoming "tonal" (the field of relativity). The Upanishads refer constantly to the unmanifest emerging into form.

At the conclusion of the movie *2001: A Space Odyssey,* the fetus appears, floating in space, representing new birth. In this same fashion, the role of this inaugural Aries phase is to emerge and claim its space. This "spring babe," this Aries-ness, personifies the stage of the *cosmic infant* that has just been birthed.

What I am addressing here is the pure Aries archetype, not necessarily the Aries Sun sign people that you may know. Very few of us have one prominent solar influence; as I already mentioned, most of us have three, four or even five signs strongly represented in us, blended into a complex astrological mosaic—a part of this, two parts of that.

In other words, don't be confused if Uncle Bud is an Aries Sun sign and exhibits qualities associated with several other signs. Other tendencies might also be due to past-life experiences (a topic too broad in scope for this book). Remember that in the initial points I made regarding differences between the signs, I said that each of the signs react greatly as an outgrowth of its preceding sign. Even though Aries is the first sign of the zodiac, this still applies. The *"circle of zoo animals"* (the zodiac) is an endless continuum. Aries bursts forth from this void and simply represents the joy of living. "You can *have* the nothingness of Pisces," exclaims the hard-headed Ram, "I want to be somebody!"

This eruption into being can barely be contained by the newfound "limited" body in which Aries finds itself. The newborn's needs are immediate and must be satisfied. Hungry to confront challenges and impossibly impatient to carve its own autobiography, the pure innocence of the youth cries for intercourse with its immediate environment.

Aries lusts to experience itself.

To be mired down into analyzing all the intricacies of any given situation would inhibit their ever-maiden voyage. Being the germinal phase of the zodiac, they need to constantly blaze new trails and essentially have no "past" to weigh upon them. A spark is a spark is a spark. Fires start with an explosion.

As a fire sign, Aries has a great need to act. Fire signs, including Leo and Sagittarius, need to express themselves vitally and energetically. They usually have strong spirits and exhibit a zest for life. And because of this, they can either incite or singe those who linger nearby. Being the first sign of the zodiac and starting off the first quadrant, Aries is also a cardinal sign. Cardinal signs are leaders and naturally generate activity. Putting the two qualities together, cardinal fire, the Ram is a "leader of fire," or full of inspiration. They are the pioneers, and have difficulty yielding to anyone else's lead.

Consider just a few of the people who exemplify this Arian essence: Catholic mystic St. Teresa of Avila, western spiritual leader Ram Dass (formerly Dr. Richard Alpert), mythologist Joseph Campbell, psychologist/author James Hillman and President Thomas Jefferson. All were certainly pioneers in their respective fields. The clarity of vision that each proffered provided a blank canvas upon which the richness of their daring life encounters were sketched. Oh, and let's remember to include René Descartes, Michelangelo and Leonardo da Vinci.

Each had a need to dive directly, unimpeded into the unknown. Ram Dass once lamented that he felt that he was not contributing to the world by not battling on the social front of the 60's "revolution" since he was sequestered in an ashram and deep in meditation for months in India. Then he realized that his Arian nature had, in fact, placed him on the very forefront of the "battle for evolving consciousness." He was actually on the front lines sparring with his (and our collective) demons. Keeping with the archetype, he trail-blazed the path to higher consciousness for the growing collective of the late 20th Century.

The Aries archetype needs adventure and dies along the roadside if not regularly exercised. Aries dogs, for example, need to run more than other dogs. Aries is ruled by the planet Mars, and Mars rules the muscles of the body. Those energies need to be expressed and worked. It's their instinct. Muscles need to be flexed. *Give me some elbow room!*

As Mars ramrods through space
There's simply not time
For long stories of pain
Whether witless or sublime

Is now not the time
So endless and clear
Refusing tangled misgivings
Burdened with fear

Everything about Aries is protuberant: their behavior, jutting foreheads, strong angular noses, bumping their heads all the time, and so on. Aries is like the hood ornament on the front of a car: out front. No need for a brake pedal, just the gas. No "please," either. Can we just get going? Sometimes others view Aries as rude; and sometimes they are! *Let's get on with it; life is happening out there!* No need for rear view mirrors; they know where they've been.

To capture the feeling of this irrepressible energy, we might take a look at the lyrics of Aries John Kay, lead singer of the band Steppenwolf, in the song "Born to be Wild":

> *Get your motor running,*
> *head out on the highway.*
> *Now, we're lookin' for adventure*
> *or whatever comes our way.*

And then again, from their song "Move Over":
> *Yesterday's glory won't help us today.*
> *You wanna retire?*
> *Get out of the way.*
> *I ain't got much time.*
> *The young ones close behind.*
> *I can't wait in line.*
> *Move over!*

Because this initial astrological prototype lives more in the "here and now" than any other, it is quite possible that they have a greater capacity for actual memory than any other of this select dozen. After all, they are more present during each and every moment. They simply will not accept obstacles that could hinder them from direct experience. When Arians have something to say, they say it. If they have something to do, they do it. If their path is strewn with thorns and vines, they get a machete and chop the dang things down. Simple.

> *The advantage of Aries energy is that it sticks up for itself.*
> *The disadvantage of Aries energy is that it sticks up for itself.*

Many people find Aries to be difficult to deal with because of their "self-oriented" tendencies. Sometimes this principal sign just can't understand that others have differing opinions, tastes or viewpoints. But, if you think about it, Aries don't usually criticize others. Rams usually get irritable when they view others as slowing them down. It matters little whether it's intentional or not. They aren't taking a philosophical stance; they just want to keep moving. Too many times we take Aries too seriously. And they won't be quiet if life's intersections are jammed up with the indecisive and the overly cautious. After all, almost every Aries knows exactly what they want and can't grok others who don't.

I recently spoke with an Aries client who has a considerable degree of experience in the realm of the occult. She more than dabbles in the art of Shamanism. I asked her what she does when she encounters "dark" forces in her journeys. "I just brush them aside and keep on moving past them," she said.

It is easy to get exasperated with this fire sign. The Ram can be demanding and want everything their way, and right now! This is precisely why the Ram is their chosen symbol. If they want something, they simply dive right in and grab it. (Yes, former NFL color analyst John Madden is an Aries: "Boom!") This does not infer that all Aries are bulls in china shops; it simply refers to their bold, pioneering, assertive and direct character. They often think that others are unadventurous, too cautious, too obtuse, and simply afraid to fight or confront. Another Aries client of mine was leaving my office after a reading and said, "I'm not sure what planet is banging into what, but I sure do feel better!"

Aries has a strong sense of self. This first sign must be careful to remain self-oriented as opposed to selfish. When Aries becomes too self-focused, they need to activate the Libran side of themselves (the sign opposite Aries) and become more considerate of other people's needs.

The following true stories exemplify this tendency:

An Aries father once promised his young Cancer daughter a puppy from the animal shelter. You can imagine her uncontained excitement when she arrived at the pound and was drawn towards all the pathetic creatures in their sad cages, yearning for a home. She instinctively leaned towards choosing a soft, fluffy animal that needed her mothering instincts. Abruptly, her Aries father chose a young, healthy Beagle puppy for her. After all, he was a hunter.

The little girl was emotionally crushed, not having been given a choice as promised. She had no place in her heart for this dang Beagle. When they got home the little girl went crying despondently to her mother. Naturally, the Aries dad was perplexed and irritated. He had gotten her a dog, just as he said he would. What was the problem?

Once I took an Aries date to a party. She wanted to go home early because no one was fawning over her. She got her wish.

These stories, of course, are not indicative of all or even the majority of those strong with the Aries archetype but sadly, they do represent how some of them are simply incognizant of other's needs. This myopic viewpoint can be an asset or a liability and is usually both.

Aries don't barge into life's arena intending to aggravate, spite or hurt others, yet at the same time, they are gladiator-like. It's simply how they move: from "A" to "B." They aren't *necessarily* trying to run that stop sign; they're simply moving forward and the stop sign cramps their style. Known for being fearless and brave, there's a strong degree of childlike naiveté thrown in, to boot. It comes with the territory.

In a sense, there are no "others" with Aries. This archetype is about "self-ness." It represents the emerging self acting with singular purpose—that is, *self-actualization.* By no means does this indicate that they are snubbing others, it simply attests to the fact that before you can have duality you must first have a self to refer to, a starting point.

It is critical that we understand the relationships between all the signs and their polar opposites across this heavenly loop. The pairs. The polarities. We learn much more about a particular sign by comparing and contrasting it to its opposite sign. And in the case of Aries, the sign directly opposite to them is Libra. The Aries-Libra axis has much to do with identity. Aries finds verification about the self from their very self, whereas Libra finds much of its identity from combining with another, actually using their partner's banter as a sounding board. Much more will be detailed regarding these pairings as we go along and you will find amazing parallels amidst the six major polarities of the basic zodiac. Aries is not a sign of broad consciousness; it's a sign of *self*-consciousness. And I don't mean bashful or shy, but rather, awareness of the self. Me!

Aries is imbued with a refreshing childlike (and hopefully not childish) nature. Quite often we feel good just being around their vivaciousness because life somehow feels simpler, appears brighter and is more directly accessible.

> *"It is said that we are all seeking a meaning for life. I think that what we are really seeking is the experience of being alive so that our life experiences on the purely physical plane will have resonance with our innermost being and reality, so we can actually feel the rapture of being alive."*
>
> — *Joseph Campbell, The Power of Myth*
> *(Aries mythologist, 1904-87)*

Simplicity is the Arian way, impatiently deflecting all complications and entanglements aside. Aries lives freshly, alive, unfettered, exposed and vulnerable to the moment itself. Because of this urgent debut, the Ram is enamored with its very quintessence and a common refrain is heard: "What about me?" The other eleven signs of the zodiac have natures that are more complex, for better or worse, and can't even "remember" what it was like to be Arian; just as few of us can remember our formative years.

Non-Arian signs tend to fill their lives with emotional baggage, getting tangled with others. Not this sign.

Every spring around March 20, as we traverse the sign of Aries for 30 days, I notice how many people say things like, "I want to buy myself something," or "What about me for a change?" "I think I'll take a bubble bath and spoil myself." At this time, our focus is quite naturally on ourselves. After all, how far can we get without this "self"?

It is much easier to understand and appreciate the "infant-like" nature of this state after you have sojourned down the zodiac a ways and looked back at the clear, uncluttered slate that is this primary sign. This by no means indicates a lack of anything, save complexity.

The Arian state is simply simplicity.

The essence of this archetype yearns for life's exciting offerings. Is it accurate to say that the other signs take this elementary status for granted? Many of us could learn a great deal by taking more notice of this stimulating original stage. If the Aries people you know don't exhibit such a self-oriented bent, it is most certainly because of other outer planetary placements in their charts or an overall convoluted blueprint.

It's no wonder that people with strong Aries energies tend to love babies. Usually you can spot an Aries quite easily from the eager, innocent and guileless look in their eyes. The simplicity of Aries is even noticeable by their youthful look.

More so than any other sign besides Gemini, they usually look the youngest physically well into their senior years. Innocence is their norm. Usually, they're not "up to something"; what you see is what they are. *You got a problem with that?*

Raising an Aries child with caution is not advisable even though they are constantly bumping their heads from being so headstrong. They are made to jump first and think about it later, or maybe just jump first. Too many of them have their mettle dampened by parents laden with more cautious energies such as Taurus, Cancer and Capricorn. Rams need to learn about life by using their instincts and that means bumping into things headlong. How else are you going to find out how well you can do in a demolition derby unless you go out and crash into something? It may be unsettling to tamer souls in the family but that's their *modus operandi*. What else can the first sign do? Wait around for instructions and approval? It doesn't work that way. Fire bursts into flames!

Let there be light!

These young-spirited forms carry the unadulterated initial seed that is bursting forth, like a tender shoot. Other people can see their innocence and that can take them far. It has been written about for ages that Arians tend to prevail upon others with their demanding needs. I've found that while this can be true, most others tolerate Aries' behavior simply because their intentions are benevolent.

Because of their natural candor, Aries commonly gain another's trust immediately. Many times, to Aries' dismay, they trust others too easily and that can lead to many a rude awakening. However, Aries get over it quickly. They operate from inner spirit, undiluted, and are not to be encumbered with the contents of other people's thoughts or feelings. This is largely true for all three fire signs.

Since it's simply not their nature to recognize anything foreign from their own Arian nature, by default they can't be contaminated. Foreign objects (others) are beyond their purview. So, what's there to be afraid of? Is this fearlessness or naiveté? Thank goodness we have a sign like this that is so self-assured, straightforward and unfettered.

The early signs of the zodiac are mainly *personal*. Generally speaking, as we orbit further around the zodiacal circle, the mind tends more towards the transpersonal. Early signs are not unsure of themselves; we can't really say that a baby is unsure of itself, can we? Yet, like a fawn, their developing legs tremble beneath them as they acclimate to the world.

Aries can seem very sure of themselves even at times when they are not as "on target" as they'd like to think. Sometimes this straightforwardness can make them sound really confident when, in fact, many times they tend to oversimplify issues. The myth of Aries is that if they keep on diving headlong into situations, they'll come out ahead. (Aries rules the head.)

> *The report card for Aries receives an automatic A+;*
> *it succeeds due to its very existence.*

I once had a great friend, a 93-year-old Aries man who has since passed over. Hazen was a fine southern country gentleman. Any time we discussed anything that involved complications in any form, he'd always say, "Nah, I ain't gonna fool with it."

Taurus: Terra Firma

Taurus glances back over its shoulder and shushes the Aries infant: "Be patient, someone is coming to feed us soon." With this sign, overall consciousness expands. The focus is not just on the self, but what the self *has*. The Taurean baby has grown from the initial stage of Aries and beyond the simple fascination of *being*. It provides substance to what Aries has started and secures the new self *to* the self.

Seated in the second position of the zodiac, Taurus represents the human stage of the *baby*, where he or she notices their substance and the immediate world around them: their nose and toes, smells, tastes, touch and such. This is where Taurus gets its association with *value*: what it has, it possesses. That is why this sign is commonly associated with money, collections and liquid assets.

As we get deeper into astrology, we find that the real essence of Taurus is more than just material possessions. At heart, it's about *self-worth*. So many times my clients ask me about their financial situations. Although I am not a financial astrologer, I do find that the flow of money to each of us is usually directly related to our sense of inner worth. (Isn't that the same principle upon which Napoleon's Hill's bestselling book *Think and Grow Rich* is based?)

The Taurus archetype values the status quo, often to the detriment of refreshing change or relief. We can now see how this second sign provides us with the basis from which further zodiacal signs emanate, by being rooted in the earth.

The topography of the Taurean landscape is generally populated by simple, pragmatic, sober-minded and unassuming souls. A vision of a cozy Hobbit hole comes to mind: one of furry feet seated comfortably facing the fireplace, with pipe in hand and a hot cup of tea. There's really no reason to complicate this sign or to even try. Thank goodness that this one sign of the zodiac likes to keep it simple, full of the bounty and richness of potential that their well-tended soil promises. It is elemental and earthbound.

The key to understanding one born with a large imprint of the Taurean archetype is that they satisfy themselves with simple stimuli: a simple flannel shirt, a worn threshold, a walk in the woods, their favorite old dog, and so on. Usually, no sign lives in a quainter world while still being content. They enjoy the musky, unrefined and untainted aromas of life. The sign of the Bull can be one of the most unpretentious signs of the zodiac, typically passing on flights of fancy.

Can you see now how it differs from its predecessor, Aries? Taurus needs to dig in and nestle. Their essential nature is fastened together with sturdy nuts and bolts.

They are not to be budged.

Another Taurean trait is their hospitality. I've noticed so many times when I visit a Taurus' house how they make me feel comfortable. Their pantries are stocked with food and drink. They assure that you are okay then they go off by themselves. This is not antisocial behavior; it's their way of avoiding chaos. They've provided for you; now let them be.

When you deal with those having strong Taurean characteristics, never hurry; it makes them ill at ease. Just like the tortoise in the famous *Aesop's Fable*, they'll get there when they get there. They move slowly but surely so don't rush them.

In astrological lingo, this sign is fixed and is an earth sign. Since the element of earth is the most practical, fixed qualities and earth together in Taurus results in dogged determination. If a Taurus is available to do your tedious taxes, you would be well advised to take them up on it. They'll persist until it's right and save you every penny they can. Taurus' persistence, which is their strength, is oftentimes their weakness because they never know when to give up; therefore, we have the Taurean myth: *If you push long enough and hard enough, you'll get what you want.* Not necessarily!

How can anyone complain about Taurus being stubborn when its essential "job" is to implant itself into terra firma? The essence of Taurus is stability, resoluteness, solidity and backbone; moored and secure.

Where would we be without our sturdy foundations?

I just read for a Taurus woman and together we unearthed much about her past from her natal chart. She asked me if she could lie on the floor while we talked because it made her feel comfortable and secure— a natural position for this sign. For Taureans, movement is destabilizing, unsettling and nerve-wracking. "Please, just sit down," you might hear them say. Taurus does not like change or movement; change implies upheaval.

This second sign is usually quite visceral and sensuous. Because they can be hedonistic, they know how to satiate the senses. If a Taurus is cooking, you don't want to miss that meal. Since they have such a great appreciation for the earth and all things from it, they are the sign that loves food—preparing it, smelling it and especially savoring it.

This second sign of the dozen can be very possessive. Similar to the sign opposite the zodiac, Scorpio, they can view their loved ones as possessions. As you can imagine, this doesn't often turn out well; in fact, many Taurean parents can be very difficult. Oftentimes, I consult with offspring of this sign only to find out that their Taurus parent simply could not see anyone else's point of view, period. If there is too much Taurus energy in the natal chart, the likelihood of this occurring is much greater. It's really not because the Bull wants to be difficult, it's just that, you see, in their fixed perspective, you simply must be wrong if you dare to disagree. I always remember of the popular TV character Archie Bunker when I think of the shadow side of Taurus. "Stifle yourself, Edith!"

I really don't believe that God said, "Hey, let's make a stubborn astrological sign today!" Why then is it common for Taureans to insist upon their point of view? It's because other points of view threaten their comfortable, stable, rock-solid perspectives and thereby cannot be sanctioned; they're forbidden. The unyielding posture of one's arms crossed at the chest is signified by the Bull; their unyielding stance is their power.

True subjectivity cannot address objectivity,
for objectivity doesn't yet exist in the zodiac,
and the Taurus archetype is purely subjective.

The primal urge toward security and safety is typified in Taurus and Cancer, which is a major reason why these two signs often marry each other. For Taurus, it's no doubt the need for physical security; for Cancer, it's the need for emotional safety. Taurus is sensible, sturdy, sure and sane. No sign gets more irritated than Taurus when it comes to others who act willy-nilly or overly excited. If someone's chart tilts towards being capricious, Taurean planets can balance and rescue the entire chart.

Taurus' job is to settle down and provide substance and sustenance. They view overly exuberant people as being somewhat out of control; thus, we see that the zodiac's most patient sign follows immediately after the most impatient, Aries.

All signs react against or grow out of the previous sign.
That is one of the main defining motivations that inform each sign.
The very archetypal basis of Taurus is to stop Aries from flying off the handle.

The simplicity and purity of the rudimentary sign of Taurus provides a solid armature upon which other planets and signs can build. Taurus adds great stability to whatever is affixed to it.

Like Aries and other early signs, Taurus shares many childlike qualities, although these traits are often hidden and hard to see beneath their rough-and-tough exterior. Agree with it or not, because of Taurus we now have a rock bed basis from which to grow. The branches of the tree of humankind can only extend as far as the Taurean roots have dug in.

How appropriate that The Buddha was born to the archetype of Taurus and is commonly portrayed affixed to the base of a Bodhi tree, where he is said to have received enlightenment. That's what I call a strong Taurus: roots and branches (microcosm and macrocosm).

Paradoxically, The Buddha reached to the stars by
surrendering his desires to the earth.

We know that closed systems don't survive. While it is the nature of Taurus to keep things simple to the point of "no change" or even rigidity, they *must* push beyond their own comfort zone to grow branches and reach towards the Sun for nourishment. It is their existential nature to stay dug in, to bore themselves into a specific spot, but will they end up being buried there? Look at where former Iraqi President Saddam Hussein (a Taurus) was finally captured: hiding in a hole in the ground! Another Taurus, Adolf Hitler, spent his dying moments sequestered in an earthen bunker. Thankfully, most Taureans are not dictators.

On the other hand, the stability of Taurus can provide comfort and strength. I am reminded of my Taurus grandfather, Giosue. He sang Italian tunes to me when I was very young. He was truly present with me as we relaxed there amidst the sweet aroma of his pipe tobacco and homemade wine. There was no one else in the world but the two of us. He knew how to make me feel special, as if I were the only thing that mattered. He was solid, strong, certain and humble. There was nowhere safer to be than planted upon his knee.

> *That is the beauty of Taurus: they are present*
> *(a great trait of the early signs).*

I once read for a Taurus woman whose chart indicated that she was going through a phase of exciting, enlivening energy from the planet Uranus. Uranus is one chaotic planet, especially to someone who is not comfortable with change. Our discussion revealed that she was not feeling these new erupting energies; however, she claimed that her children were "driving her nuts." I knew that I was onto something when she said this.

Uranian energy explodes unpredictably from within us to crack our old crusty shells of stagnation. It wants us to renew ourselves (which is really coming from our inner self). This woman's story implied that she was not in touch with the spark of change coming from within; instead, she had been projecting the source of the disruption onto her "unruly" children. As a way of blending the energies of Taurus and Uranus,

I suggested that she put on some old clothes and take the kids outside to play in the mud; play in it, throw it at each other, roll in it.

She called me a few days later, stating that I had "solved all of her problems." She explained that she and her children had never had more fun than they did playing in the dirt. With that comment, I knew that she had overcome her own paralysis. I went on to explain that her problem appeared to be related to her children but it really wasn't; it was her own inner child that needed to be liberated. This is a typical story of the Taurean archetype, as well as a little bit of an explanation of how Uranus works.

You have to water a plant or it will die.

After 30-some years of working within the Western system of astrology in which Taurus is traditionally ruled by Venus, I am now convinced that it is instead ruled by the Earth itself. The Earth ruling Taurus makes much more sense, although this assertion begs many questions—especially since it is the central point around which all the planets appear to rotate. *It is the fixed center,* therefore it doesn't move (just like Taurus).

I can tell you with great certainty how common it is to hear earthy Taureans talk about their love of gardening, landscaping and getting their hands burrowed into Mother Gaia.

As we forget about Venus
Turning our eyes towards the earth
We can now see quite clearly
The true home of our birth

Taken for granted
The very base of our race
Its comforts so strong
We even forget we're in space

At one time I did a lot of astrological readings at festivals in an old amusement park. A local dentist stopped by every week to trim the hedges on the vast property, all at no charge. (A Taurus working for free?) His natal chart showed five planets in Taurus. He was financially well off and kept quite busy during the week, and on the weekends those hedges were all his! They grounded him.

It should come as no surprise that many rough-and-tough actors in Western movies were Taurean, such as Jimmy Stewart, Anthony Quinn, Henry Fonda and Gary Cooper. Isn't it apropos that the late comedian George Carlin was born to Taurus? Was he not known for his down-to-earth, no BS humor? This is one of my favorite Carlin lines, which shows how Taureans can really simplify matters:

Carlin once said that a glass is not too full or too empty, it's simply too big.

With other Taurean artists, we see the gutsy, intimate side: Stevie Wonder and Steve Winwood with their funky styles, the overwhelming vocal powers of Roy Orbison and Barbra Streisand, Pete Seeger's grassroots protests, Willie Nelson's simple-hearted vocals, James Brown's soulful grunts, the scat-singing of Ella Fitzgerald, and let's not forget the raw purity of Joe Cocker. By expressing themselves from that primal place, these Taureans stir that same marrow within us and inspire us at an instinctual level.

Taureans, like Arians, are known for being very convincing. Commonly, their arguments are overly simplified. One reason they are so persuasive is that they identify closely with the basic instincts of life. Psychologist Abraham Maslow, known for theory of the hierarchy of needs, had his Sun and Moon in Aries with Venus and Mars in Taurus: survival, food, drink, safety, sex. Yes, Sigmund Freud was a Taurean; on the shadow side, so were Vladimir Lenin and the Reverend Jim Jones.

Not all Taureans are dictators or military leaders, but they are all fixed and persistent. As a matter of fact, I have found that a common thread amongst enduring politicians like Mitch McConnell, Nancy Pelosi and Dick Cheney is having a strong vein of the Taurus archetype. Agree with them or not, they can take the punches. As history has shown, crowds identify quite easily with these leaders' simple, strong messages. Look at what Oscar Schindler, another Taurus, was able to do during World War II through guts and perseverance. Taurus is one stubborn sign. Don't play "King of the Hill" with them unless you want to be toppled.

The Civil War had an immediate turning point once Abraham Lincoln appointed Ulysses Grant to be in charge of his military forces. True to his Taurean instinct, Grant simply dug in and outlasted his opponents. Look at the sieges of Vicksburg and Petersburg. In Vicksburg, he relentlessly bombarded the Southern forces that were dug into the hillsides of that Mississippi river town and starved them into surrender. At Petersburg, his army dug a huge underground hole beneath the Confederate Army's position and dynamited them to kingdom come. (Oh, then much of his army got trapped and died in the very same crater.) Sooner or later, the enemy had to eat and was forced to surrender. It was a bloody war of attrition. No one can win a siege war against astrology's Bull.

This first quadrant of the zodiac—Aries, Taurus and Gemini—is all about the "stuff" of man: the primal elements from which man issues forth. This second sign of the zodiac fits comfortably in the middle of this quadrant. Taurus clearly is a "self-oriented" sign. It is simple and untainted with the complexities of embroilment with "others."

The theme of the six polarities of the zodiac becomes more illuminated now. Taurus: my stuff, my value, my self-worth; the opposing sign of Scorpio: our stuff, our values, my self-worth *when I'm with another.* We're beginning to see how the poles work. This wreath of symbols is one marvelous tool and is truly magical when understood.

The gritty sign of Taurus can only do what it does; it is simply not able to remain self-contained if it is expected to extend far beyond its comfort zone and get tangled up in complications. Self-containment is the goal. Yes, this sign would be easier to deal with if they were less stubborn; on the other hand, we can certainly appreciate their resoluteness. As previously stated, their implacable nature is an outgrowth of and a reaction to the explosive birth that commenced in the initial stage of Aries.

I once had the great fortune of working for a wonderful film producer, the late Ellis Dungan. He was a sure, tough and grounded Taurus and we made many types of films together—the majority of them were industrial or educational in nature. One day, we were filming for a coal company near Pittsburgh, Pennsylvania, a project that took us 800 feet underground. The atmosphere inside the mine was claustrophobic and eerily dark; we were tightly surrounded by mud and damp, seeping walls. While Ellis and I took a lunch break that day, I watched him plop down on his camera case, comfortably nestled in the mud. As we passed around pepperoni rolls and warm cans of soda, Ellis hoarsely cleared his throat and said something I'll never forget.

"Ain't this the life?" he commented in his gravelly voice, grinning from ear to ear.

Ellis was in his element.

"Hell, boy, when I go, I'm gonna die with my boots on!"

Gemini: Isn't That Interesting?

Gemini is perhaps the most enigmatic of the celestial dozen. The fleet-footed domain of Gemini is ruled by the planet Mercury, the messenger god. Being a mutable sign (dispersion and exchange) and an air sign (thought and mind), Gemini is always on the lookout for novel ideas. This ever-youthful archetype is clearly astrology's most curious. This stage of man represents the *toddler* who has learned to walk, explore and communicate. And boy does it ever! "Why, why, why?" Gemini has an incessant need to discover the new. As a matter of fact, it seems like those with strong Gemini influences use the word "interesting" in every other sentence. Since all signs are an outgrowth of the previous sign, the Twins have become restless with the ever-stable fixed sign of Taurus that preceded it.

> *The secret of Gemini is that it must escape*
> *the staidness of Taurus; therefore, it must explore.*

What happens in this capricious, critical third stage? When we examine the outgrowth from Taurus to Gemini we can truly appreciate the drastic changes taking place within the zodiacal embryo of the first three to four signs. Gemini clearly represents a magical, alchemical transition. Gemini is the coming out party.

All twelve signs have a job to do; Gemini's is to scout for new information. Its recon mission scans everything, for the whole world is its theater. Even when a Gemini is captivated by a new sighting, it is already restlessly looking for the next fascination; then their mutable air energies urge them to develop the ability to communicate, gather data and spread the word. As one of my Gemini friends answers when he sees my name appear on his caller ID, "This is Gemini Central Control!"

If you really need to keep a secret, this is most likely the sign to keep it from for they love to spread the news; in fact, Geminians are walking encyclopedias and natural broadcasters. The Gemini archetype's purpose or *daimon* (when motivated by a spiritual force) is gathering information. It's almost as if this very stage separates subjectivity from objectivity; thus, the Twins. Just as Taurus needs to dig in and root itself, Gemini needs to levitate, spread outward and explore its surroundings. *Everything is so interesting!*

Those with large doses of Gemini energy are known for their extremely youthful appearance, such as Bob Hope, Michael J. Fox, Nicole Kidman, Mike Myers, Johnny Depp and Elizabeth Hurley. Like Aries, Gemini also looks younger and stays thinner into their elder years. It's no coincidence that early signs of the zodiac look youthful.

Puck, the sprightly character in Shakespeare's *"A Midsummer Night's Dream"*, and Tinkerbell, the whimsical, luminous fairy that flits about in J. M. Barrie's *Peter Pan* are good examples of the positive archetype of Gemini: cheerful, friendly and lighthearted. Those with significant Gemini traits in their charts have little interest in docking themselves in any port; after all, they have just sprouted from the most sedentary of signs: Taurus. As we've seen with Taurus, the motto is "stick with it" and "git-r-done." That's simply not Gemini. Gemini does not fly backwards, for doing so would return them to the status quo of Taurus and death (in their minds).

It has taken me many years to solve the riddle of this sign and it's no wonder. It's the sign of the trickster. Does it surprise you that the voice of the cartoon characters Bugs Bunny, Daffy Duck, Sylvester and others were all of Mel Blanc, a Gemini himself? Geminis are at home in their intellectual sand box; they're playful. *Can't everyone else just loosen up a little?*

Much of the Gemini's sprightly nature is inspired by the changeable, curious messenger planet, Mercury. Astrology's psychopomp has no time to tarry.

> *Mercury's path is so quick*
> *Burning close to the Sun*
> *Curious here and then there*
> *Never resting, never done*

Never taking a stance
Not able to cease
The next act will be better
What did I just see?

Isn't it fitting that the former Beatle, Gemini Paul McCartney, once stated that his favorite Beatle song that he had penned is, in fact, "Here, There and Everywhere?"

The archetypal Gemini darts about in a horizontal fashion. What does this mean? Just like the honey bee, Gemini is usually bouncing from blossom to blossom because they get bored easily; a little taste of this and little taste of that, and then it's time to check out the next garden. Geminis, like water bugs, skitter along the surface and don't want to be "bugged" about it, either. There's much more of the whole pond to investigate. They are "lateral learners." This is why Geminis are frequently mislabeled as being shallow. They don't have much choice; it's their nature to seek a breadth (not depth) of knowledge.

Each stage can only do what it can do.
They naturally do what they are meant to do.

It's like a king who orders his Gemini subject to explore and report back his findings—the perfect job for Gemini! When he returns, he has lots of *interesting* facts. Certainly, this new information will be of use to his king, but it is not within the Gemini archetype to take a position or to evaluate whether or not another army looks threatening, or to advise whether to get busy building walls or more weapons. Gemini's job is to be the scout, make a fact-filled report and get ready for its next exciting mission.

Thus, one of Gemini's greatest secrets is this:
since they are geared to learning a little about a lot of things,
their overall knowledge can be seen as superficial.

They can't be tethered if they are to keep soaring and investigating, so, by definition, they aren't anchored. To be anchored is to die. Geminis simply can't invest the time to dwell on any one subject for too long. They are the butterflies of the zodiac. They are not made to take a stand any more than their wings can accept being pinned down.

It's almost as if their persistent need to explore nullifies their ability to slow down and have more than one brief sniff of the roses. Even so, remember, no sign is cursed or without free will. In order to counterbalance this restless personality, what must be found in the remainder of a Gemini's natal chart are earthy forces such as other planets in Taurus, Virgo or Capricorn, or a significantly placed Saturn (according to a professional astrologer's assessment.) If these are present, they can go a long way towards taming and anchoring the restless Gemini. These additional grounded energies can alter their temperament, giving them the additional capacities to compile, analyze and utilize information before floating over to the next novelty.

When we examine the sign opposite of Gemini, we see how this antsy quality permeates the entire Gemini-Sagittarian axis. With Gemini, it's about what *I* have found to be of interest mentally. With Sag, it's more about the collective mind, how *we* think and communicate.

The Twins don't care about staying put until they absolutely have to— and even then, only for a moment. There does come a time when they yearn for a place to alight. Keeping with the duality theme of the Twins, Gemini misses the comfort and stability of Taurus yet needs to keep on gallivanting. Geminis bemoan this inner conundrum, since their archetypal drive impels them to keep stocking their mobile library. It's off and exploring once again, over and over; more intelli-nectar to collect. It's no wonder that the Gemini myth is, "The grass is always greener on the other side of the fence."

Many times I observe when I am with Geminis that they can be very subjective yet, a millisecond later, this fickle sign can objectify you as if you're being viewed under the lens of a microscope. Quite often, they switch back and forth rapidly between subjectivity and objectivity, interrupting you and *themselves* mid-sentence. It can be hard to know where you stand (or where they stand). That's because everything is an interesting idea to Geminis. They objectify everything, including themselves. When they view something subjectively or try to take a stand, they get wobbly and backslide on what they just said and quickly disown it. The Twins!

This third sign of the zodiac is usually in a big hurry. Its sense of "this" is constantly being overlooked in favor of "that"; thus, Gemini often finds itself living in the future.

Heading back home once from a European vacation with my family, my Gemini mother already had her house keys in her hand as we were boarding the airplane in Rome, Italy.

The Twins are even mystified by *themselves*. I have asked many astrologers and read many discourses on this tertiary sign and have never been satisfied with any explanation I have heard as to *why* the Twins are their symbol. Why did astrology's founding powers-that-be assign a split icon to this singular sign? Yes, many authors will tell you that they are like two people. *But why?*

After many years of obsessing about this sign, I believe that I have discovered another reason that makes the Twins tick. For one Twin to learn about itself, it must compare itself to the other Twin (subjective-objective). This vacillation between the Twins is necessary; one Twin doesn't even know about its very existence without this comparison. When the Gemini has fulfilled its cosmic duty, satisfying its archetypal impulses, the resulting entity is broader, more conscious and capable, and has emerged from the seedling that was initially sown in Taurus. Gemini gets spent, retreats back into subjectivity for security, gets bored, runs back out to objectivity . . . and back and forth it goes, a constant fluctuation between duality and non-duality.

It seems as though Geminis have nowhere to anchor themselves . . .
because they don't!

Gemini has learned that Taurus' pure subjectivity can only persist for so long. Eventually, man's vision needs to widen as the objective world unfurls and becomes more and more elaborate and fascinating. True objectivity cannot exist without something subjective with which to compare. That's the Catch-22 of this sign; the butterfly can't land and it can't keep flying forever. I have talked with many Geminis who simply cannot rest. Their wandering mind—the chattering "monkey mind"—is in control.

As the embryonic stages of Aries and Taurus are transcended, the Gemini's inner self naturally evolves outwardly. The basis of all three of these early archetypal forms is purely subjective and self-oriented.

This third stage is where the inner self (or whatever you want to call it) starts to sense <u>personal consequences.</u>

Since the element of air has just been introduced, there is not yet any true individuality of "self" to speak of. Immersed in this unbounded dimension of thought, Gemini is unaware of itself. In this undifferentiated world of pure concepts, one idea has the same value as any other. This is why everything is so equally interesting. Eventually, amidst Gemini's stream-of-consciousness narratives, the very act of being objective *forces the observer to detach and define itself as separate.* As we look closer, we start to see that it was all part of the zodiacal plan. Suddenly and *inadvertently,* consequences have materialized but as of yet, there is no actual faculty in which they can be borne; therefore, they recoil. Consequences are just another mental concept, not matters that they are prepared to own and react to just yet.

This third stage is not completely ready for "results." It's in a perpetual pre-result stage, and that can be daunting. There are ramifications to being a sovereign, stand-alone entity. This is not what Gemini bargained for. No wonder it's time to slip-slide away!

Once again, because of the dual nature of the Twins, they vacillate between subjectivity and objectivity. The consequences of taking a position affect objectivity. Werner Heisenberg's *Uncertainty Principle* tells us that mere observation of an object affects that object and blurs the distinction between the two. By definition, this quantum effect evinces that there is actually no such thing as true objectivity.

The Twin's real duality is the interplay between unawareness and awareness.

Interacting with Geminis can be a bewildering experience. Many times, and rightly so, others take offense at something the Gemini says or does. Are they being critical or are they just joking? That question constantly haunts their companions. We can see this circuitous dynamic unfold if we look closer. Many times the Twin is accused of being critical when all they are doing, in their opinion, is "verbalizing passing thoughts." No other sign can say things that sound so stinging or negative while insisting on disowning them immediately. What was a subjective observation is masked as an objective remark. Or, was it? AC/DC. Yin/Yang. Spin the karmic wheel, and off we go again.

Watch closely and you'll see how those with Gemini tendencies take serious matters lightly and light matters seriously. The trickster can be quite dizzying yet their sharp tongue can still cut deeply.

Those strong with the Gemini archetype feel constant pressure from others to grow up and *feel* in a deeper way. But the mental vagabond needs to soar and can't if he's towing anybody's emotional baggage around, even his own. Oftentimes, Geminians get themselves into serious jams because they can project their own lack of feeling onto others. They're young and spirited and are not made for the political correctness of life's complexities. They prefer to say what they have to say and get on with things. *Life's a vacation, right? Geez, let's just have some fun!* As I said, the point is that they're playful and one can't always play.

Gemini is commonly described as slippery and evasive. They don't intentionally start out to be this way but can quickly become so. This third sign can only listen to subject "A" for so long before itching to get onto subject "B." Never mind if they have finished "A" or not. Those with strong Gemini influences commonly have ten books open at once and seldom finish any. They skim only what they want from each. It's just not their nature to finish anything.

Anything goes! The Twins are the flirts of the zodiac. Flirting affords exploration without commitment. Flirting with what? People, ideas, lifestyles, beliefs, anything and everything. Nothing is off limits to this sign's curiosity. Even when a person has only one or two planets in the sign of Gemini, they can often be quite kinky sexually. Since they can *imagine* anything, that means they can *consider* anything. Why not? Their minds have no limitations. Isn't that one reason why Geminis are so much fun? When you are around them, life simply feels lighter and more limitless.

Did you ever try to corral liquid mercury on a tabletop? It's not that Gemini is trying to avoid something; it's simply that they will not be pinned down. You'll seldom get a direct answer from this whimsical sign. You know what I mean if you've ever seen Gemini trickster Bob Dylan being interviewed. He seldom, if ever, gives it to you straight. He'll even contradict himself then deny it. The reason is that giving an answer implies taking a position and taking ownership, which would be limiting. Taking a stance belongs to Taurus and Gemini's opposite sign, Sagittarius.

The following quote is an actual response I received from a 50-something Gemini client. As I was asking about her sense of being elusive, I used the image of a taffy pull to describe the constant conflict between the Twins. "A taffy pull is a good way to describe it," she said. "I've struggled with identity issues since I was a young child. And only now am I getting any inkling of my true self. The only way I've held it together for this long was to slip away. I became quite adept at looking a person right in the face and convincing him or her that I was right there in the conversation, but not even being anywhere close."

ADHD is a common prognosis for children with a surplus of this fleeting archetype. It is often sad to see a free-ranging mind constrained and regimented by the education system and put on medication. The Twins are simply not made for concentrating on one thing at a time. They're great at multitasking and thrive on change and variety. You'd be surprised how many times I've been able to give great relief to people who have Gemini emphasized in the career section of their charts. I often recommend that they get a second job: one serious, one for play. They simply can't believe it. What a relief it is for them; oftentimes they've been forcing themselves to choose one over the other and hadn't even thought about a dual option.

Unlike their predecessor Taurus, who is adamant about maintaining the status quo, the Gemini spirit cannot and should not be restrained. Gemini rebuts Taurus by saying, "You're not going to smother me anymore!" As we are seeing with all of the signs, each must transform into the next. Taurus can't stay put anymore. The Bull has to give it up, let go, get out and expand its environment. The Gemini chick hatches from its shell only little by little. Complete emergence from its confines comes at the end of the next sign of Cancer. It seems that every sign has an unconscious premonition of what's to come next.

Cancer-time means it's time to leave the cerebral sandbox behind.

The first quadrant of the zodiac has fanned out into a beautiful mini-spectrum. Its varied colors are on display. The diversity of astrology's first three elemental signs has revealed sub-cycles of God's plan. The zodiac is symbolic of His inherent interconnected wisdom. It is exquisite.

Only now can we look back, even a little ways, and appreciate Aries and *the self*, Taurus and their *substance*, and Gemini's ever-active *mobile library*. Thus we see that the first quarter of the zodiac represents the very substance of evolving man.

Still, there is much more to learn about the Gemini trickster, astrology's kaleidoscope. Without this blithe, curious stage of Gemini, man would be much smaller, confined to fewer options and less able to *navigate*. The thrust of the Gemini archetype is its obsession with epistemology, the study of *how* the mind learns. That's their job and they're darn good at it, too. Gemini gives us lightheartedness where there often is somberness. A refreshing view of the world has replaced the "same ole, same ole" of Taurus. Everything changes. How interesting.

Cancer: Splashdown

Few would attempt to chronicle the one-way virtual trip down astrology's birth canal . . . but I am going to try.

The shock of us instantly finding ourselves in a completely new environment is very disorienting. The previous cerebral stage of Gemini has no choice but to let go and dive into the strange new waters of Cancer. This new water-world proves to be both overwhelming and refreshing.

As we leave Gemini, we cross into the second quadrant of the zodiac. This quarter represents the developmental stage. Each quadrant starts anew with the next cardinal sign. Cancer, our second cardinal sign, takes the lead but this time by its *feelings*. This is the womb, as the blossoming mind of Gemini now finds itself gestating in Cancer's cauldron of emotion.

Each of the first four signs is a pure representation of astrology's four elements, yet Cancer is located in the second quadrant. From where does this "self-oriented" sign get its urge to develop the self, which is what the second quadrant is all about? It is imbued with a need to gather the self and start to give it shape and definition. The Twins were happy to collect all types of data. If Gemini were allowed to continue its endless explorations, much progress would be scattered to the wind. Cancer provides the repository in order for integration to start taking place.

Similar to Taurus, Cancer's urge is for safety and security. El Toro needs *physical* security; for Cancer, it's *emotional* security, which is derived from the comfort and protection of the family unit. In fact, these two signs are one of astrology's most common couples and best matches.

Without a doubt, the transition that takes place between Gemini and Cancer is the most dramatic in the zodiac. The reason why is because the relative "evolutionary" distance that is to be traversed by Cancer between embryonic Taurus and expressive Leo is immense, indeed. That's just the way it is.

The magical transformation of each archetype into the next is true alchemy. Cancer has grown weary of Gemini's endless roaming. The intellectual, butterfly-like stage of the Twins morphs into the next sign of the Crab. Now, evolving man yearns for the safety and comfort of a home. Cancer can no longer remain at arm's length to its environment, as was the case during Gemini's objectifications. The duality has ended.

With this new unification, the simple freedom that was enjoyed by Gemini's detached perspective must be offered as a sacrifice into the Cancerian broth. Much like the way early NASA flight capsules (named *Mercury* and *Gemini!*) splashed into the sea, Cancer is now swamped by a vast ocean of overwhelming sensations that lie beyond the thinking mind.

With these sensations comes personal responsibility
and the gift of the water element: feelings.

This newfound emotional consciousness of the young spirit is born in this fourth stage and has much with which to contend. Cancer must become more than just a collection of thoughts. It is starting to recognize that it is a being and with this realization, its survival instinct kicks in.

Now, the Cancer must actualize itself and does so by naturally aligning with the archetypal pattern that is deeply embedded in its core. It's as if their ancestors are speaking through their very DNA; this is why Cancer rules family, lineage, history, tradition and one's roots.

As this sign slowly gets acclimated to its unfathomable and frightening realm of feelings, it is predisposed to stay close to the mother and the nest. The self is expanding and the family becomes its extension. True individuation doesn't begin just yet. The growing self still needs to identify with the pack yet Cancer has managed to transmute the aloofness of Gemini into the intimacy of emotions. Remember, Cancer is ruled by the changeable Moon. Cancer, being a water sign, can be very challenging because the feelings of any two people become so intertwined. These ebbing sentiments bring ambiguity as to who is who and what is what.

Cancer's paradox is between being mothered and being motherly.

We are dealing with the element of water for the first time, and water connects us to one another, like it or not. As Cancer grows, it absorbs and assimilates this new elemental force; it has to figure out how to take on water without drowning. The process of self-development eventually weans the babe from the breast.

What exactly is Cancer stirring up in her cauldron? Aries' *self,* Taurus' *stuff,* Gemini's *ideas . . .* and now add to that Cancer's *feelings.* In this primordial soup, the four elements are combined for the first time. Cancer's survival instinct may be the strongest of the zodiac, which it is why it's now charged with vigilantly nursing this concoction into a viable, stand-alone personality. She settles atop her eggs ever so gently in the nest.

Cancer not only introduces water and emotion to the group-self but starts to understand its world by exploring its way with its *feelers*—thus, the Crab. This crustacean is crafted to move sideways, cautiously, and ever-ready to defend. To the evolving self, treading water is the first priority before worrying about propelling forward—symbolic of gaining emotional strength.

Despite its emotional nature, don't be fooled; the Crab also has a tenacious side, thus the large claws. In general, Cancer cares little about what someone else says or does in deference to how someone makes them feel. "If Mama ain't happy, ain't nobody happy!" *And don't mess with her family, either!* Nothing is more essential and intrinsic than one's family, especially one's mother.

The self is learning to open up and reach out—hence, becoming vulnerable. This is not easy. It's no wonder that Crabs are often hypersensitive. Cancer has taken on a lot. Look at what they have contributed to the collective being: family, traditions, emotions and love.

The world is truly hydro-powered.

Like it or not, this is the stage where the inner self has personal consequences that land squarely in their laps, and there's no more getting around it. Consider these song lyrics by Moonchild Cat Stevens:

Oooh baby, baby it's wild world.
It's hard to get by just upon a smile.
You know I've seen a lot of what the world can do
And it's breaking my heart in two.
There's a lot of bad and beware.

Cat's admonishment is not based on logic; it is *felt*. Few signs are more intuitive; there is danger out there. Ramifications from dealing with the "outer world" are now here and can no longer be avoided. No wonder the Crab wants to crawl under a rock and hide. The Cancer chapter of man is very, very touchy.

Outside threats to their safety are one thing;
the inevitable severing of the umbilical cord is another.

Cancer unavoidably finds that disconnecting from the mother coincides with the development of the self. And, that just might be too much to bear at this stage.

Keeping with our theme of the twelve stages of man, Cancer epitomizes the stage of the *pre-teen*. Can't you just feel this from Cancerians such as Robin Williams, Tom Hanks and Tobey Maguire? Remember comedienne Gilda Radner? How about these other Cancers: Lindsay Lohan, Liv Tyler, George W. Bush and the biggest grown-up kid of all, Bill Cosby. You get the point.

Not surprisingly, Princess Diana Spencer, another Moonchild, had a doe-like, vulnerable look in her eyes. Archetypally, she *was* "the innocent." Her mass appeal was directly related to our collective desire to protect her or recapture our own innocence. When Diana was viewed alongside the stoic royal family, the scene presented us with a visual juxtaposition that clearly made her "the people's princess."

Conversely, many Cancerians have a hardened veneer that shields a soft inner core, which is how the symbol of the Crab was intuited. Hard outside, soft inside.

To truly understand the nature of this fourth sign, it behooves us to gauge how far the zodiac has unveiled itself thus far. If we zoom out and look at the broader picture, it becomes very clear. Aries is necessarily wrapped up within itself, absorbed in *being*. Taurus is preoccupied with being grounded. Gemini is busy exploring. Cancer is charged with blending it all together. The pure elemental stages are ending.

Cancer safeguards its creation as it attempts to ensure its inclusion and security within the family walls. In a similar fashion, Capricorn, its opposing sign, is ultra-protective of its *position in the world*. These two signs are the most cautious. Cancers, known as the worriers of the zodiac, often carry fretful looks and furrowed brows. Many look older than their age.

This shaky insecurity comes somewhat naturally. The Crab needs constant reassurance from loved ones, as the self is still in the process of formation. The blurred line between the self and the family can either foster or hinder Cancer's independent growth. People with strong lunar qualities can be quite irrational. No wonder—the Moon rules Cancer and the Moon is downright crazy. Loony! It is a very difficult planet to describe. Even so, the Moon is the second most important planet in all of our charts, symbolizing our emotions, lifestyle and habits.

Consequences are part and parcel of this stage of evolving man's progress. These "new" consequences can seem to be out of proportion to what feels fair. Fair or not, Cancer finds itself at a critical juncture; at some point they have to accept responsibility for themselves.

The asylum of personal boundaries is just being established.

This is a challenging transition but if Cancerians succeed, this rite of passage results in self-reliance. Hopefully, Cancer starts to own their personal consequences and we're all better off for their efforts.

These lunar matters are universal in nature, often resulting in make-or-break situations. In the natural world, all young must eventually leave the nest, even to the point of the fledgling being rejected. Only human beings tend to hold onto their young for whatever reason. Is this evolution? The success or failure at this stage is decisive and either launches the success of the offspring or can signal its demise.

How many times do we find ourselves holding on too long to something or someone to our detriment? It's the same dynamic. Dependency and attachment issues affect *all* of the signs; Librans tend to be too attached to their partners; Virgos, to their work; Capricorns, to their positions, and so forth.

The Moon's rulership of Cancer helps to clarify much of this ineffable archetype, including its moodiness. Though often unwarranted, Cancer is prone to feel like no one loves them. This hypersensitive sign is apt to see the world through a binary filter: "You love me/you don't love me." So, why are Cancers so moody? Because that's how they feel, that's why. Feelings don't follow rules.

Remember, we never see the other side of the Moon except indirectly. Likewise, in this all-too-common manner, we frequently have to guess how someone else is feeling. Not with Cancer; their feelings are worn on their sleeves.

The Moon has a warm and a cold side. It nurtures yet it's dependent. It's tender but can be off-putting and cold. It comforts yet it can be inconsolable. And it loves freely yet can slam its doors shut.

The mystifying Moon, earth's nightlight, has many facets that keep astrologers rubbing their chins. When a person's Moon is "troubled" in the natal chart or by transiting planets, logical antidotes are seldom useful. Someone simply has to find a way to make the Moonchild *feel* better.

> *Oh Moon, shine brightly*
> *Constant yellow glare*
> *Your shadow side escapes us*
> *Somehow, that doesn't seem fair*
>
> *Our partner in dark*
> *Dim visions of old*
> *Tied to you still*
> *From the bygones we hold*

Just as the Moon gets its light from the Sun, Cancer gets its sustenance from others. This sensitive water sign needs plenty of reassurance, as they are just learning to summon strength from within. Even so, they will be the first ones to offer *you* emotional support if you need it. Like all the water signs, they are commonly sympathetic and warm. That's what makes this sign so endearing; they're naturally kindhearted and supportive.

Cancer gets much of its identity from its mother or other nurturer. This is why the first question I ask my Cancer clients is, "Growing up, how did you get along with your mother?" If the answer is positive then I'm usually not too worried about their sense of self-worth.

The Crab's intent is to hold the family unit intact. Lunar types are the matriarchs of the zodiac; this is equally so with the male gender. They greet you with a warm smile and insist that you be well fed. They ask how you are feeling. They're sensitive to every nuance of your life, will listen to your smallest distress and will not mock you. Cancer is the sign we go to when we're hurting.

Because of the Cancer archetype, we have a place to go on the holidays.

However, Cancers who didn't have a healthy bond with their mother usually have emotional development that is thwarted. A Cancer child needs lots and lots of TLC. A careful analysis of the natal chart bespeaks of one's upbringing: only then can an accurate assessment be made of how this human seed was nurtured (or not). What's most critical is how the Cancer *perceives* his or her upbringing.

Few signs have such capacity for sympathy and empathy, especially towards children. Without this maternal instinct, no species would survive; yet it must be remembered that this archetypal stage is still symbolically "young" and has needs of its own. Cancer is a "give and take" sign. These seemingly oppositional urges can result in a detrimental codependency if one is not careful. So, this begs the question, "For whom are they doing it?"

Usually it's for the benefit of both parties and there are strings attached. At times, conflicting messages are received by the child. The shadow side of a Cancer parent can make it seem as if their actions are intended solely for the benefit of the child; however, upon deeper reflection, *it is often apparent that the child has become obliged to meet the needs of the parent.* Many of these children simply cannot free themselves from this implicit contract. In actuality, many of them end up "raising" their Cancer parent.

It's all about the comfort of having someone with us.

We continue to see this paradox between parenting and being parented. No sign can be more of a nurturer or more needy than Cancer, and may be both at the same time. Cancerian parents must be careful to not enable their children to become overly dependent. Will they allow their children to take their lumps or will they buffer each of their falls? Care must be taken to not project their own fears and hypersensitivities onto the child, imagining that every scratch is traumatic.

The archetype of Cancer represents the act of mothering and being mothered. The mother and child are inextricably connected—again, the Cancer paradox. Like the splitting of two cells, the cells are separate entities but are there really two psyches or still one? In general, no sign suffers the loss of a mother more than Cancer. Attachment to the matriarchal figure can be kept alive like an emotional phantom limb.

The real jeopardy of the Cancer archetype is this: if the child does not feel that his or her needs were met, he or she can become prone to blaming someone else for their emotional pain (usually the mother). And if that happens, the scapegoat becomes *the* reason that their life is a flop. If this projection is not checked, the child is tempted to prevail upon others, thereby eluding the consequences of their own actions. Sometimes they are so overwhelmed with the harsh realities of growing up that they simply don't know what else to do.

The myth of Cancer is that if it surrounds itself by enough buffers, it'll be okay.

Whether it's actually true or not, Cancers can feel abandoned emotionally. If so, they can resort to using guilt and manipulation to get what they feel they need and, in extreme cases, can lodge themselves as an emotional thorn in the side of the family—a centerpiece of need around which the whole family must revolve. While these situations do occur, it serves to underscore the utter importance of early bonding with a Cancerian child.

The Crab cannot be assuaged at the logical level; it just won't work. Keep in mind that to Cancer, keeping the emotional umbilical cord intact is a *life or death matter*. As the Cancer phase is mastered, what once was unthinkable in terms of cutting the cord must now occur. Just as the Moon reflects sunlight, emotional maturity must be echoed back from the maternal source to the child.

The embryonic signs of the zodiac are beautifully childlike and innocent. They are also the most refreshing because they reside closest to the source—or, the sign of Aries. Cancer displays its cardinal strength as it defends its family. With a moat of protective water (amniotic fluid) that surrounds the castle, they keep the threatening wolves at bay. Cancer is the second cardinal sign. Unlike the cardinality that was expressed earlier in Aries, it's not full of fire and brimstone; it works instead with love, patience and tenacity. The inchoate Cancerian is stunned by the surprising effects of feelings that seemed to originate from the "outside world" as it exits Gemini. For the first time it becomes aware of its vulnerability and impermanence. It's no wonder that it seeks the haven of the pack.

The Crab must flex its strength and take advantage of its powerful claws. Eventually, Cancer outgrows its natural timidity. It has eclipsed Gemini's over-intellectualization and has contributed a meaningful new realm of emotion to the overall collective because water is the elixir that holds the entire zodiac together. Truly, "someone had to do it," and that someone was Cancer. Armed with each of the four elements, evolving man grows more powerful and complete—capable of defending our families and land from our foes, real and imagined.

Cancer has a great allegiance to its roots. No sign is more loyal to their particular lineage and is more patriotic. The oft-used phrases, "My country, right or wrong!" and "Love it or leave it!" are clearly based upon these principles. Born on the fourth of July, the United States, a Cancerian country, is also known appropriately as the "melting pot." When viewing America through an astrological lens, you can see the Cancerian motif, for better or worse. The USA's maternal instinct is evident as we sweat over the safe return of our soldiers. Whether it's a little girl stuck in a well shaft or a boy floating loose in a hot air balloon, we cannot rest until our family is back within the fold. The patriotic rallying cries heard during the Civil War, the World Wars and 9/11 were Cancerian to the core. Certainly other countries feel the same way but Cancerian countries have a heightened sense of homeland and an urgency for "homeland security."

However, we also suffer from the dark side of the Moon. Just as the Crab has a soft underbelly, we are inclined to be provincial, keeping our boundaries closed. Americans have a strong proclivity towards hearing what it wants to hear, turning a blind eye to the real facts. We are too easily appeased by political buzz phrases, paying a stiff price just to feel safe. Safety, however, is often illusory.

This Cancerian vulnerability is exploited when the government misleads us using threats to our security, such as warnings of the proliferation of Communism in Vietnam and Korea, as well as weapons of mass destruction in Iraq and elsewhere. Many a clever politician has taken advantage of the USA's Achilles' heel: the fear and the desperate need for emotional shelter.

On the morning of September 11, 2001, terrorist-controlled airliners crashed into the Twin Towers and the Pentagon, monolithic symbols of American stature and strength; for evermore, we are vulnerable. The planes shattered the Crab's outer protective shell. No longer would two huge oceans and two vast friendly neighboring countries keep us safe. What else could a Cancerian nation do? Create the Office of Homeland Security.

Having an inherited and informed yet scattered self from its Gemini predecessor, what was once quite amorphous is now taking shape. Now, through its fierce need to mother and gel the family together, Cancer has reconciled itself. The end of the Gemini frenzy and the desire for home and stability has placed life's components directly into Cancer's oven.

The time has come to open the door.

Gemini remains equidistant from all things—even itself—because it has no point of reference, but by the nature of emotion, Cancer feels others and therefore by default feels *itself;* thus, subjectivity is introduced. Birth has occurred. This new archetype discovers that the world is both close (self and family) and far (non-self and non-family). We finally have a point of reference.

The zodiac's fourth stage may very well be the most difficult to master. With love and attention, nurturing and care, Cancer has been baptized in water. What once was a bewildering sea of emotion has now become familiar.

These lunar traits are quite difficult to understand but who wants to live in a world that is entirely rational? So often we have heard from our wisest teachers that the mind is both a great servant and a terrible master. We have our answers: they encourage us to "get out of our minds," "follow our bliss," and "listen to our hearts." We intuitively grasp this truth. The throbbing heart is our God-guidance-center and from it is heard the "still voice within."

As Helen Keller, a highly evolved Cancerian, once said:

> *"Security is mostly a superstition. It does not exist in nature, nor do the children of men as a whole experience it. Avoiding danger is no safer in the long run than outright exposure. Life is either a daring adventure, or nothing. To keep our faces toward change and behave like free spirits in the presence of fate is strength undefeatable."*

Leo: Everything's Fine

Each sign blossoms from the accomplishments of the sign before it. No sign can do it all; each has a specific assignment in this exquisitely complex zodiac. The evolving stage of Leo is becoming independent, confident and self-expressive.

Individuation of the self has begun.

The Leo world is an outgrowth of the cautious, uncertain state of the Crab, which is closely aligned with the mother, family and nest. At this point, the Lion, like the archetypal Hero (the quest for transcendence) goes it alone and tests its own strength. It reflects back to Cancer, "What are you so worried about? Get out there and take command!" Symbolic of the *first ego*, Leo must survive! This is the first time in the development of the zodiac that the self gets a solid, complete and independent view of itself. This fifth chapter represents a significant boost to the development of the evolving self. Even so, just below the surface, Leos still carry the insecure Cancerian imprint, which they cannot afford to acknowledge (but other people recognize it nevertheless; that's the irony).

The main thing to know about the Leo archetype is that it has transcended the Cancerian need to carefully guard itself, which kept it safe and secure. It was necessary for Cancer at the time but now, by expressing itself, Leo releases its own power into the jungle of the world and enlarges its sphere of influence.

When an astrologer sees a chart laden with Leo traits, it usually means that the person has great skills of expression. Whether that is found in music, art, theatre or other means of elocution, the Lion roars. (We'll see later how its opposite sign, Aquarius, expresses itself via the group. "Leo = *I* express" versus "Aquarius = *We* express.") Just as Cancer tends toward the tentative, Leo is quite the opposite, commonly putting on a dramatic display. The Sun does shine brightly! When faced with conflict, no longer vulnerable to paralyzing introspection, Leo says, "I can't be the problem! It must be *you!*" Quite a shift has occurred. Right or wrong, "defense of the self" has to happen.

This is one of the most decisive shifts in the evolution of the entire zodiac.

Each sign of the zodiac becomes satiated with the "games" of the sign that precedes it. The very survival of the evolving self is threatened if it doesn't reinvent itself. This is what propels one archetype to morph into the next. Leo is as much of an extrovert as Cancer is an introvert.

Placed smack-dab in the middle of the second quadrant, the Leo archetype is all about developing the self, the theme of this quadrant. This is the first sign that becomes comfortable dealing with personal consequences. The Lion takes on all comers and courageously invites consequences. Leo benefits from receiving feedback; some might call it the *limelight.*

With its proud mane, Leo starts to give form to the advancing entity developing in the lower half of the zodiac. Another of the self-oriented signs, Leo does much to cultivate its sense of self as it nears the transition from "self-orientation" to "other-orientation."

The tentative inner self is busy proving itself, just as a teen does, but doesn't want anyone pointing that out. *Who are you calling a teenager?* Well, in the scheme of things, Leo symbolizes the stage of the *adolescent.* Bear in mind that Leos often behave more confidently than they really are. Teens must go through this ritual of growth where they have to push themselves past their comfort zone. It takes a brave soul to leave the cozy nest behind.

A common by-product of this critical rite of passage is that the Leo-teen knows everything, right? Just as with teens, it's often hard to tell them what's best. Nevertheless, by hook or by crook, the Lion finds its mettle. The Cowardly Lion in *The Wizard of Oz* personifies this developmental stage (actor Bert Lahr, who played the lion, was born a Leo). He started out faint-hearted but quickly found himself to be the bravest of the group. The teenager finds self-regard through self-expression.

No sign is as magnanimous, loathing pettiness and poverty of spirit. It's not their nature to engage in gossip for they see the poison that it inflicts upon another's dignity. This fiery sign produces people with infectious personalities who are larger than life, such as Mick Jagger,

President Barack Obama, "Magic" Johnson, Mae West, Jennifer Lopez and Arnold Schwarzenegger. They think big and are usually able to execute their plans on a grand scale. The noble Lion radiates warmth and color into his surroundings in a generous, robust way. Leos are naturally the centerpiece of the family; the hearth.

"Respect" is their keyword. This solar-powered sign *commands* respect. In the work place, being respected and appreciated is more meaningful to them than a paycheck. They absolutely must be appreciated and if they're not, the mood for the day won't be pretty. Because of their buoyant nature, it's rare to see Leo get upset; however, if you want to see someone blow...

What comes to mind is the famous factory scene from the movie *Norma Rae* where actor Sally Field stands up defiantly and inspires fellow workers to shut down their machines. Galvanized by her inner strength, everyone finds the courage and dignity to stand up for their rights and unionize. This is the Leo archetype at work; its fire will not be extinguished.

Pride and dignity for all; that is Leo.

So what exactly does this archetypal energy have to say? What compels it to speak? Self-expression is its highest goal. Only when you express yourself do you distinguish yourself as an individual. Leos naturally project themselves into their environment and are baffled when other signs are reluctant to speak up for themselves. Confidence and self-assurance result when the self is expressed; the Sun *must* shine.

Solar flares and Sun spots
Yes, we know that you're there
Granting us light
Enthroned in your lair

Leaving no doubt
To those far below
But what lies in the havens
Of your hidden shadow?

By standing on Cancer's shoulders, they have not only gained separation but have also won self-hood in the process. This proud fire sign has benefited greatly from the fight that Cancer won in the trenches of emotion. Leo's newly found self is a wonderful thing. Whether this triumph leads to humility or vanity is up to Leo and is greatly influenced by a number of factors, including a preponderance of planets in Leo, their role models and upbringing, and other astrological markers. A healthy ego is necessary for all signs, and this sign has built-in self-respect. Leo Robert De Niro's famous line from the movie *Taxi Driver*, "Are you talking to me?" is quite indicative of Leo indignation at being dissed. But, Leo must be very careful to not totally identify with the self-concept (or, ego); that is the key. While confidence can be the Lion's strength, overconfidence can bring about their downfall.

All signs have a built-in pitfall, and Leo's is possibly the most dangerous. Whatever could that be? Getting lost in their own melodrama. If success at this stage is not accompanied by a sense of perspective and a modicum of modesty, Leo can end up becoming a legend in its own mind. This imaginary realm can somehow seem finite to them, as if there's only so much love, attention or accolades to go around. Such a worldview can make one unnecessarily competitive and prone to projection, imagining that others are trying to steal their thunder, even when it isn't true.

It is Leo's nature to find a dominion to oversee. If they're mopping the floor, it's *their* floor, an extension of their ego. Individuation is blooming in this stage; however, they must avoid their shadow side, which can see the world from a "me versus them" viewpoint. If they fall prey to this, they can have difficulty complimenting someone else or even acknowledging others in the same room.

No sign deludes themselves more than Leo.

Commonly, Leonine types tell me how they are constantly confronted with competitive, jealous people. Few signs experience jealousy more than Leo. Many times, this is a projection. For better or worse, all signs tend to see others just like themselves. As if living in a house of mirrors, the signs of Cancer and Leo can become too wrapped up in themselves, seeing only their reflections. It is all too tempting for budding Cancer to feel that everyone is here just to make them feel better, and for the Lion cub to see others as simply members of their audience. These understandable but immature tendencies must be outgrown. Success of the self during the Leo stage must be attained. This is a crucial turning point in the development of evolving man. Failure at this stage is not an option, as all ensuing signs will build upon the individual who is being strengthened in Leo . . . and it must not lose!

While it's true that Leo likes center stage, the reason is because garnering adulation assures them that they're okay. But exactly how much do they need? The shadow side of Leo simply cannot get enough attention and always yearns for more. Note some famous Leo figures who don't seem to suffer from low self-esteem: Madonna, Barry Bonds and Andy Warhol. Some find it difficult to step down from their thrones: Fidel Castro, Jerry Falwell, Bill Clinton and Martha Stewart. What they really need to do is find approval from within; that's the remedy.

Leo's favorite word is a four-letter word that starts with "F": FINE. Leo's standard response to just about any query goes something like this: "Oh, I can handle it . . . it'll be *fine.*" Listen and you'll hear it often. There is a "fine" line between cockiness and confidence. Nevertheless, no matter how you slice it, this kind of swagger is a great gift to have. Astrologically, all of this is leading to the maturation of the consummate human being.

As the zodiac's twelve archetypes evolve, each naturally relies on their main strength: Aries comes out and fights; Taurus digs in its heels and roughs it out; Gemini accumulates data and won't be pinned down; Cancer tenaciously guards itself and its nest; Leo puffs up its chest and rises above. That's what Leos do; they rise above. If it comes across as arrogant, so be it. It's their job to protect the ego at any cost.

Leo's victory here is not only that pride and dignity are achieved for the individual; this process has also contributed to the progress of the collective self. Eventually, this solar sign transcends the limitations of its own story and discovers that the world is, in fact, infinite.

As John Lennon sang in *Instant Karma:*

> *Who in the hell d'you think you are?*
> *A superstar?*
> *Well, right you are!*
> *Well, we all shine on*
> *like the moon and the stars and the sun…*

Because of the advances made in this stage, the self now feels strong enough to stand alone. That's one huge step! We all gain greatly from Cancer's higher octave of Leo. A feeling of impeccability has been gained because this proud sign has found self-hood by looking within. When you have the power of the brilliant Sun behind you, that's a lot of wattage.

All signs present their own unique problems and carry the seeds of their own solutions. And for Leo, it's to not back down, compromise or acquiesce; it's to uphold the self, to stand up proudly and hold its ground. Leo is a fixed fire sign – its flames keeps on burning.

The self is now well on its way towards refinement in the final "self-oriented" sign of Virgo. Each of astrology's twelve stages tends to stretch their own limits until such a time comes when it can do so no more. Universal intelligence itself somehow takes over and a quantum leap is made to the next sign's dimension.

> *It is not possible to separate ourselves from the*
> *collective needs of our human race.*

Now, Leo's spirit eventually infuses into evolving man. An ornate crown of gratitude should be awarded the noble Lion as a giant step for mankind surely has occurred. (Yes, astronaut Neil Armstrong is a Leo.)

Virgo: Beyond the Call

Virgo brings closure to the quadrant of the zodiac pertaining to development of the self and the "self-oriented" signs. Evolving man now prepares to bridge himself to the "other-oriented" signs. Virgo not only invites personal consequences but absolutely *thrives* on them. We continue to see how much one sign differs dramatically from the sign before it.

Reacting strongly against Leo, Virgo wants no part of self-promotion or accolades; that's for show-offs. Usually shy, they prefer functioning behind the scenes. This humble sign voluntarily forfeits their share of life's rewards in deference to the needs of others. They never ask for more than their share, if even that. Virgo says to Leo, "Get that lampshade off of your head!" Nothing embarrasses Virgo more (and they do get embarrassed by many things) than having their horn tooted, no matter who's doing the tooting. They insist that their work speaks for itself. They are self-made people and expect the same from others.

When something needs to be done, Virgo just does it.

If you want to hire someone, find a person with strong Virgo qualities. Usually, without even investigating further, you'll have made the right choice. Not only will they get the job done right, they don't want any recognition. Many of them work overtime as a matter of course and with a strong sense of dedication. Few signs are as skilled. Virgos are usually spot-on in whatever they attempt to do. Their strength lies in their ability to use their sharp, analytical minds to differentiate this from that. Their nature is to find out exactly what is "broken" and fix it. And they can't stop from fixing it, down to the very last detail; and herein lies the catch.

If you want to find something wrong with anything, you usually will.

Because they are quite perfectionistic, persnickety, prudent, puritanical, picky and just plain particular, they inevitably fall short of their own standards of impeccability. Keen use of this archetype's perceptions differentiates what is fixable, what is not, and what is fine as it is.

The first five signs of Aries, Taurus, Gemini, Cancer and Leo have had the "luxury" of being self-oriented. The early stages *had* to be this way. Yes, the sign of Virgo also belongs to this category yet they can no longer afford to be so self-absorbed. Their job is to bring self-involvement to an end. Virgo is the culmination of this process as the zodiac prepares for its orientation toward the "other."

This transition from "self-orientation" to "other-orientation" must occur.

Perhaps this is why Virgo bumper stickers say, "No more whining!" The proverbial buck has to stop here because symbolically the stage of the young adult is about to take its show on the road. This tough earth sign can become intolerant of people who complain without trying to dig themselves out of their own self-created predicaments. They'll be glad to help you (mutable earth = lending a practical, helping hand) but you have to exhibit at least some willingness to help yourself, or their support quickly wanes.

Virgos are also very tough on themselves, to say the least. Their natural toughness can result in great self-discipline. In fact, some of the greatest athletes of all time are Virgo Sun signs known for their skills and endurance, such as the phenomenal Lou Gehrig, Jesse Owens, Rocky Marciano, Cal Ripkin Jr. and Lance Armstrong.

Many times the Virgoan archetype regards emotion as weakness. Why is this? Emotions are sloppy, gooey things, aren't they? They're simply illogical. *Star Trek's* Spock was the epitome of this Virgoan archetype. Many times Virgos unknowingly substitute their feelings with a black-or-white mentality brought on by their left-brained, logical approach. (This is a very important point.) Likewise, Virgos can get so out of touch with their feelings because they act from "shoulds" instead of how they feel.

Virgo is as rational as Cancer is irrational.

Those strong with Virgo energy simply have a hard time with emotional expression. This is sad yet common because these folks are usually salt-of-the-earth type people: honest and hardworking. They'll give you the denim shirt off of their backs, but not in exchange for a sob story; they don't want to hear it. They can't even hear their own. Therefore, what does this forecast for their inner child? Just how much sensitivity will they show others or themselves?

Virgos were made to bring an end to all of the whining that went on earlier in the zodiac; however, the Virgo archetype often goes too far, mistaking emotional expression for whimpering. If you don't tolerate complaining in yourself, how can you tolerate it in others?

This leads us to discuss the theme of "self-criticism," Virgo's middle name. They don't need to hear any criticism from you, even if it is "productive" or "constructive"; they hear it enough from themselves. Now we see a hint at the Virgin's secret:

They don't want others to see how critical they truly are.

This archetype magnifies imperfections, often seeing only what's wrong, broken or missing. Most Virgos are very careful to not criticize others but their nonverbal critiques are still heard loud and clear. Virgoan parents care for their children largely by providing food, clothing and shelter but since they usually don't give themselves a break, they can become too critical and intolerant of their children's normal behavior. It's all too common for their children to grow up feeling like they can never do anything right. This is not a minor issue. Unknowingly, the child enters the fussy Virgoan realm where all things are dissected and mended. This tendency towards being too critical can easily extend to all of their personal relationships if they're not careful. Their natural nitpicking is better off left at the office, else they can end up leading a lonely life.

Note how archetypal Leo says, "Nothing is wrong with me," then Virgo comes along and specializes in finding out what's wrong with themselves and, many times, with everybody else! This is just one example of the fluctuating tendencies throughout the zodiac where themes seesaw between adjacent signs. As a result, mankind is diverse and well rounded. This evolutionary stage, now self-contained, becomes so because it tempers itself as it answers the call of introspection. Through this effort, Virgo obsesses over the purity of perfection.

Most people need a long time to address and come to terms with inner imbalances. It can be shocking to see how quickly a Virgo corrects newfound flaws. They'll have them rectified the next day and that just ain't natural! One of my clients sent an email saying: "*Any light you can shine on my progress, I will definitely review and make adjustments.*" Emotional issues generally don't get resolved that easily, so how does Virgo do it? It's called *behavior modification.* It's easy to alter how you are behaving—that is, according to outer rules—but it's quite another matter to change your basic instinctive reaction to live situations. The problem with behavior modification is that it doesn't address the underlying emotional condition; therefore, the sixth sign of Virgo commonly ends up operating like a machine. Quite often, this type operates as if life is occurring in a job jar full of tasks that need to be completed. Does this extend as far as the boudoir? Heaven forbid.

This independent sign has a lot to teach us about becoming more self-reliant. Even so, they must watch that they don't become too utilitarian. Virgo is more than a bionic man or woman. They have come such a long way past so many zodiacal obstacles and now have a difficult balancing act to perform. This is why Virgo is possibly one of the hardest Sun signs to be.

I tell my Virgo clients, "No one is following you around with a clipboard except you!" Have you ever watched a Virgo at work? Goodness, they're like a well-oiled machine, just like the NFL's New England Patriots, a team that was launched (played their first game) in the sign of Virgo. They are efficient and disciplined. No one can touch Virgo at work; they are so inspired to go the extra mile, while less dutiful souls are already clocking out.

Virgo is only doing what it *has* to do. They are known to volunteer for jobs that others would consider a burden. One of the great things about this mutable sign is that they go the extra distance, working tirelessly because they *care* so much. (That's why they often end up working in the medical field.) Because they do care so much, these perfectionists put themselves under constant pressure to be productive. On days off from work, Virgos feel awful if they don't "get something done." Still, enough is enough; they need to enjoy life now and then! I've heard Virgos say, "I think I'll take up yoga," only to follow it up by saying, "I'll *work* at it." When it comes to work, Virgo will not let you slide. Don't stop here; this is not the complaint department.

It's the nature of this ever-vigilant sign to stop the conveyor belt of life and say, "Wait! I found something wrong! How can you let something slide if it isn't right?" With all of the best intentions, Virgo can actually interrupt the flow simply by examining it so closely. And to many a Virgo, "letting things go" is a weakness that musn't be tolerated.

Contrary to Virgo, the opposing archetype, the Fish of Pisces, yields and surrenders better than any other. As discriminating as Virgo is, Pisces is non-discriminating. What's missing in one sign is commonly compensated by its opposite. Each sign contains what the other lacks. When a Virgo walks into a room, they can easily spot the differences between everyone and everything. On the other hand, Pisces sees little or no difference. *Exclusion versus inclusion*; nature always seeks balance. Virgo's challenge is to see the forest as well as the trees.

Thank goodness for the accomplishments of this sixth sign or else Cinderella would be going to the ball unkempt and unrefined. Virgo completes the bottom of the zodiac and how better to do it than to humbly take responsibility for yourself and clean up your act? (As a matter of fact, this innate urge towards purity is why so many Virgos have perfect complexions.) Even so, you can only shine your shoes for so long before you have to go to the dance. Eventually, you have to make your debut. The Virgo-to-Libra shift is huge and is one of the most underrated transitions in the zodiac.

The self is finished.

So, how does the first hemisphere of the zodiac culminate? Because Virgo has done a masterful job taking responsibility for the actions of the first six signs, we are all better off. This zodiacal chapter was simply not ready to move on until it had gone through the perfecting catharsis of the Virgin. Having concluded this critical stage, the growing self is now ready for the second hemisphere.

The icon of the Virgin was long ago revealed as the symbol of chastity and purity of *spirit* (not for its sexual connotation). This virtuous sign is built upon the noble efforts of the Lion. Virgos don't want fanfare even though they have conquered this stage of perfected man. And now, they are ready to compare themselves to all the others via the Libra scales. As I've stated before, it's almost as if deep within each archetype, each sign instinctively feels what is coming next.

In the ancient tradition of astrology, Virgo's planetary ruler has been airy Mercury. I have always suspected that this is a weak pairing; it just doesn't account for the Virgin's perfectionist tendencies. (Yes, Cinderella is nervously primping, getting ready for the ball.) Being a mutable earth sign (disperses practicality) doesn't fully explain its archetypal essence, either. These reasons simply don't provide enough rationale to make Virgo function as it does. The mandate of Virgo insists that they care and strive for purity. So, if not from Mercury or mutable earth, where do these drives come from?

. . . A minor planet or "Centaur" called Chiron, that's where.

What? Chiron? (Chiron is not technically a planet but falls more accurately under the label of a minor planet; yet, for astrological purposes, it clearly behaves much like a planet.)

However you want to classify it, this renegade rock that irregularly orbits between Saturn and Uranus is responsible for Virgo's drive. In mythology, it is historically known as the "wounded healer." A Centaur, half-horse and half-man, Chiron is known for his intelligence, wisdom and ability to teach and heal. Chiron was accidentally shot in the back of his leg by an arrow launched by Heracles. The myth tells us that the wound wouldn't heal. In a birth chart, Chiron's glyph, which is shaped like an upright key (⚷), marks the area of your life where you can heal others but not yourself; in other words, your personal wound.

Even though we associate Chiron with Virgo, there still is much to be discovered about this "planet." Chiron's (Kheiron) name was derived from the Greek word for hand (kheir), which also means "skilled with the hands." Those strong with the Virgo archetype are known to be quite adroit with their hands; many take to carpentry and manual arts because of their dexterity. (Note that the same prefix is used in the word *chiropractic.*) Many of this sign are drawn towards massage therapy. Chiron is consistently and conspicuously found in the charts of healers. Its nature is to help heal all illness.

Chiron is deeply mysterious and behaves in many ways that are unlike the other planets but is powerful nevertheless. It also seems to represent an irrepressible energy that unconsciously compels us toward our destiny. Swept away by Chiron's karmic tide, Virgo is beckoned to serve a higher order, often going beyond the call of duty.

> *Having matched you and Mercury*
> *For all of antiquity*
> *Only now does Sir Chiron*
> *Speak for your honor and purity*

> *Fooled for so long*
> *True heritage now revealed*
> *Brave and inspired*
> *What kept it so concealed?*

Another reason that Virgo foregoes accolades and attention is that they can only hear the clarion call of Chiron, the voice of caring and service itself. It's as if Chiron truly calls from another dimension. Chiron serves as a bridge between the self-oriented and other-oriented signs and also between the inner and outer planets, Saturn and Uranus. What are the implications?

> *The reason that Chiron has caused such a stir since its*
> *discovery in 1977 is that collectively we were ready*
> *for a new astrology and new forms of healing.*

The discovery of Chiron changed everything. For the first time, astrologers had a new "planet" to deal with that acted so foreign to the traditional natures of the known planets of the time. Chiron seems to call to a part of ourselves that is beyond our consensus reality.

Can you imagine the degree of risk that must be undertaken to transcend the safety and security of "self-ness" in exchange for universal principles and concern for others? Virgo/Chiron heartens us through service as we build a new bridge to the rest of the zodiac. Chiron seems to represent a major gateway to our spirituality. Chiron *is* the key.

Just as each sign morphs into the next, the Virgo blueprint, designed to heal group karma, lifts the first half of the zodiac to a new level of being. Astrologically speaking, Virgo sacrifices itself for the shortcomings of the first five signs. Without a thought of itself, for the first time, the zodiac tastes voluntary selflessness.

With the recent discovery of Chiron, astrologers need to make a new, unjaundiced evaluation of the sign known as Virgo. We must get beyond the antiquated habit of typecasting this sign simply as a perfectionist servant. The zodiac's Good Samaritans, such as Virgo Mother Teresa, should be held in high regard. Unfortunately, this is just one of the by-products that come with their territory; by not accepting praise of any type, their true value is often overlooked or taken for granted. In the final analysis, we discover that this self-effacing sign turns out to be quite the model human: caring, decent, humble and virtuous. Virgo *deserves* its accolades.

Though misunderstood for so long, I think we can finally shed some accurate light on this precise sign of Virgo. They aren't exactly supermen or women but they are definitely in a special class. Their inherent need to help, their innate yearning for purity and their need to fix whatever needs to be fixed without reward elevates the entire zodiac as it becomes more humane. Because of Virgo, evolving man truly earns its nobility.

> *"If you are humble nothing will touch you, neither praise nor disgrace, because you know what you are."*
>
> —*Mother Teresa*

Libra: Social Security

At this critical turning point of the zodiac, we now address the commonly misunderstood sign of Libra. Symbolized by the Scales, this air sign is traditionally thought to represent balance; however, upon deeper analysis, the Scales main astrological function reveals itself to be much about *comparison.* What is Libra so busy comparing? Everything and everyone. As the new self is set in motion from Virgo, it must compare itself to others. By doing so, it finds out who it is. This is truly the birth of other-orientation and the doorway to the second half of the zodiac.

The opposing sign of Aries has no need to compare itself to anyone or anything, being totally involved with the self. In contrast, Libra's need for comparison shows how the growing archetype benefits by exposing itself to something beyond itself. Just as Virgo is black and white, Libra is comprised of many pastel shades. The residual effect of Libra weighing things back and forth lends them a broad spectrum of viewpoints to consider. Gone are the days when the early signs of the zodiac tended to oversimplify.

The transition from Virgo to Libra is pronounced. This prodigious step involves transcending the self-oriented signs to the other-oriented signs, and this is major. Why else would Virgo be working so hard? Cinderella, always sentenced to the kitchen (self-oriented), now spreads her wings. She wants to party! She must escape the narrow confines of her daily drudgery. Understandably, she is still quite socially self-conscious and nervous.

As we traverse the final half-dozen signs, the evolving persona reaches young adulthood and becomes more independent. The dating-mating ritual begins, sizing each other up and making comparisons. In order to fit into society, most people must feel accepted. By contrasting our behavior and attitudes to those of others, we learn what it takes to fit in. By reflecting off of another, we learn who we are and who we are not.

Making comparisons explains almost everything about the sign of Libra.

With Libra, we begin the third quadrant of the zodiac that continues on through Scorpio and Sagittarius. The focus now is upon *relationships*. In this sector, Libra has inherited a "completed man" from Virgo, since the developmental stages are done. Fresh off the assembly line, Libra is now offered up for public consideration. In this stage, the impulse is to mix and mingle with others. The very act of socializing involves sharing feelings as well as ideas. The Libran archetype is usually not a touchy-feely sign. Only so much can be accomplished at each stage.

Can you imagine the courage needed at this point? Previously sheltered from the public, suddenly exposed, what is Cinderella to do? Compare herself to everyone else, that's what. "She is tall, I am short." "He has shabby clothes, mine are neat." "They live in big house, I live in a small one." Libra can't help but compare; this is what their blueprint dictates. Certainly, this contributes to why they make such great mediators, assessors and judges. Their social scales are meticulously calibrated to differentiate and balance even the tiniest of details, which they inherited from Virgo.

They possess a special magic. This comes from having Venus' innate gracefulness as their ruling planet and holds true for both genders. It is said of Librans, "They could charm the birds from the trees." Talk show host Johnny Carson displayed these charismatic Libra qualities very well. Rarely will you find a Libra not dressed in style (unless other planetary energies muddle their true stripes). This hospitable, charming sign is usually quite attractive, possessing smooth facial features.

Even though Venus has been the traditional ruler of both Taurus and Libra, I am now convinced that only Libra is ruled by Venus.

> *Venus is now yours*
> *All your very own*
> *The Scales now hold balance*
> *Justly, but not alone*
>
> *And with full escort*
> *Allowing none to defile*
> *The beauty in all things*
> *Behind a benevolent smile*

Being Venusian means being enveloped by beauty. (I wonder how many shopping malls would have to close if not for this sign!) They know how to beautify everything around them and are connoisseurs of anything resembling fashion, art, color and style. Venus reveals her beauty with a disarming smile. The zodiac's most glamorous and beautiful sign knows how to use what it's got. Librans can be totally disarming as they radiate Venus' captivating warmth, charm and poise. They often emanate beauty, grace and intelligence. Even if their outward beauty doesn't match Venus de Milo's, Librans still come across with an unruffled and refined delivery.

It's no surprise that many artists, as well as significant minds and personalities in our culture, are born to this Sun sign: Mahatma Gandhi, Barbara Walters, Jesse Jackson, Susan Sarandon, Truman Capote, Anne Rice, Aleister Crowley, Matt Damon, Yo Yo Ma and John Lennon. This entourage knows how to work a room!

No sign is more inclined to display their "arm candy" than this one. This alluring sign should not get lost by being fixated on how they look to others. Libra has so much to offer in terms of intelligence, gameness and elegance but they can easily fail themselves if they evaluate everything through the haughty eyes of class consciousness.

Since all signs are directly tied to their opposing Sun sign, Aries is opposite of Libra. Those strong with Arian influences are what you see; they are themselves, period. Yet the chameleon-like sign of Libra often attempts to define itself by trying to be who they think *you* want them to be. There's the catch. They see themselves and their world through a reflective mirror. Social acceptance is everything to this seventh sign and they want to be the best according to cultural standards.

Librans can't stomach unpleasant social situations or someone making a scene. Diplomacy and compromise are always their first alternatives. Even so, Libra is known as the sign that argues more than any other! Does this surprise you? It shouldn't; according to them, it's not arguing, it's *debating*. Librans are uncomfortable with the response: "Whatever you think, dear…" They want you to take the lead, only to then take the opposite track. Only by bouncing ideas off of others does Libra strengthen its still insecure and growing self.

In a perfect world, Libra is the model partner. Their considerable moxie guarantees success if they don't become too appeasing or fall for the temptation of riding others' coattails. Starting off the quadrant of relationships, the archetypes of Libra and Scorpio *need* to have partners. Librans hardly ever go into business without an associate, feeling like half of a person when unaccompanied. This is exemplary of the Libran pitfall:

Putting much of its identity into the hands of someone else.

The opposite sign, Aries, finds its identity from itself; Libra, via its partner. ("I am" versus "we are.") Libra does not "master" relationships; that challenge comes next in the sign of Scorpio where relating becomes merging; the deepening of feelings and emotional dedication. Libra starts the ball rolling by relating to others; that's somewhat different. The sign of the Scales is the most self-oriented of the other-oriented signs—the Aries of the second half of the zodiac. They are *the* social sign. No sign can counterbalance another better than Libra. It's funny but when other people sit down, Librans stand up. When other people stand up, Librans sit down, just like a set of scales and counterweights.

Libra is a purveyor of intelligence. They often represent the cutting edge of social thought (cardinal air). Did not Lenny Bruce change the whole nature of stand-up comedy? What of the huge influence that George Gershwin had on American music? Wasn't Eleanor Roosevelt a feminist role model through her social activism? How effective was Timothy Leary when he stirred up an entire generation? Libra finds its way to the head of the tribal tent. With all of their worldly accomplishments, Librans are more concerned with social norms than universal principles. Seldom will you find this sign going gray naturally or getting dirty while camping. They have reservations at the Four Seasons, thank you.

Librans admire others who are quick-witted; you'll usually find them hobnobbing with bright, astute minds. Even though Libra is a cardinal sign, it is not necessarily strong in terms of its identity; therefore, the Libra stamp can be greatly overshadowed by other planets or signs that are exaggerated in their chart. For Librans, having compensating energies are critical.

This smooth sign is all about class, both being classy and one's social class. A sound Libra personality will use his or her social acumen to assess how they measure up to social standards. If they're not careful though, the shadow side of the Libra archetype can become obsessed with one-upmanship, or "keeping up with the Joneses."

This is what occurs if the comparison game goes too far or goes awry.

All signs get off track. Libra is meant to use comparison in order to gauge what it has become as a self. Still, when the all-too-human ego gets involved, comparison can be misused and lead to feelings of inadequacy or superiority, no matter how it is masked.

When it comes down to it, they can seem coy, yet they aren't about to let anybody get over on them. Seldom clumsy or awkward, they move in a smooth, graceful way, appearing very sure of themselves. Libra, constantly paralleling themselves to others, can become prone to thinking that everyone else is doing the same—thus, another snag. The main factor that separates the evolved Librans from the others is this: *Are they for real or are they just social climbers?* This savvy sign must avoid their somewhat natural tendency to try to one-up others.

This serendipitous sign is *the* sign of the "winner" in many ways. They instinctively land on their feet. Would it surprise you to know that the majority of Major League Baseball players are born to this sign? Can you sense this winning charm (and well-known indecisiveness) in the NFL's former superstar quarterback Brett Favre?

Libra is represented by the zodiac's only inanimate symbol, the Scales. In my mind, I see two platters on the scales: one has the word "cake" imprinted upon it; the other has "eat it, too." If Libra is to remain in balance, it cannot lean to one side or the other for very long. A natural conundrum exists because of their need for balance.

Libra is not made for making decisions;
they are made for assessing situations.

This seventh sign has turned fence sitting into an art form, but that's not really the same as balancing; there is a fine line between assessing a situation and being indecisive. Their polar opposite sign, Aries, makes decisions quickly, sometimes too hastily and is seldom accused of being too diplomatic. Aries sees Libra as wishy-washy. Facing criticism, Libra still would rather be armed with all the facts. After all, decision-making is based on taking a position, and to Libra, this is too much like flipping a coin.

The Scales can be so completely preoccupied with what other people think that it can thwart its self-development. It is hard to reach beyond your own Sun sign's archetype but this echo-oriented sign has to realize that fewer people are competing with them than they suspect. If they are constantly stacking themselves up against others, it's little wonder that they feel vulnerable at every turn. Projections must be categorically guarded against. The myth of Libra is that if they are accepted by others, they surely will be okay.

The real questions for Libra are: Is this upbeat sign going to use its street smarts to excel in life or will it use its considerable charisma to pull the wool over other people's eyes? Do they glad-hand like a shifty politician or offer a sincere handshake? Naturally, all signs have their light and shadow sides. Libra is too talented to succumb to the temptations of manipulation and guile.

Libra learns and grows by comparison to others
but shouldn't become obsessed with their findings.

In the end, we find that the very act of comparison has led to an elegant state of balance. Through the successful use of the Scales, Libra has benefited greatly and has made a strong contribution to the overall evolution of mankind. For the first time within a societal context, Libra places paramount value on considering other people's feelings and has fine-tuned the art of compromise—a necessary skill for maturation.

Unlike its opposite sign of Aries, the growing Libra is aware that their actions directly cause consequences for others. Much progress has been made. Cinderella has learned to move comfortably in social circles. She's learned how to fit in and has developed refined social graces.

Yes, the obstacles faced by this cardinal sign have been considerable. This is the last real identity crisis of the zodiac. Librans finally learn that they are fine just the way they are, as individuals. During this stage, evolving man transcends self-consciousness in exchange for a larger world. The emerging self has exposed its nakedness and thereby its identity has become more self-assured.

It would be a mistake to take Libra for granted. Because of this brave, cardinal sign, evolving man now has a partner. Do you see how much the world has expanded because of this? We are not alone anymore, and this paves the way for *society and community*. On the archetypal level, the first three signs didn't have the potential to even know others existed. In the second quadrant, the signs of Cancer, Leo and Virgo were quite busy furthering the development and perfection of the self. Now, because Libra's *savoir faire* has forthrightly connected to others, because Cinderella has had the nerve to offer her identity for social consideration, we now have a world—a sparkling world in which to live and share the joys of life, with someone by our side.

> *"I get by with a little help from my friends."*
>
> — *Ringo Starr*

Scorpio: Sir, Just What Are Your Intentions?

Two-thirds of the way along our mystical ellipsis we find our diamond in the rough. Under the steady, heavy pressure of the water element, Scorpio deepens its love and summons its courage. The nature of the fixed mode constantly presses Scorpio to capture more and more meaning in the bewitching storms of love.

Even so, Scorpio has one of the less esteemed reputations in the zodiac. This intense archetype can manifest as the best of the best, or worst of the worst. People commonly take a step back when they meet a Scorpion type.

This is one intense sign.

Scorpio is at the heart of the relationship sector of the zodiac. This sign zeros in on the object of its passion. Its archetype typifies the "urge to merge." Through intimate relationships, love faces a true test, a purifying fire that may also be accompanied by anguish and dark nights of the soul. These issues are the primary reasons astrologers stay in business.

Ruled by astrology's "Godfather," the planet Pluto, Scorpio is clearly the most austere of all signs. It dismisses Libra, saying, "You may have your partner but I want a *soul mate.*" That's what this sign is all about: *emotional allegiance.* "I'd take a bullet for you, and I expect the same from you." The "love" we're discussing here is taking place in a completely different dimension than with Libra and has many of the earmarks of being conditional. New to relationships, Libra is held in disdain by Scorpio because it is seen as noncommittal. To the more audacious Scorpion, putting it all on the line is everything.

The Scorpio chapter of man is symbolic of getting married. Everything changes now that Scorpio is living for two. Matching each sign to a specific adult age becomes less and less significant as the zodiac progresses from here. Scorpio's life is now inextricably intertwined with their other half. Libra introduced us to each other and fostered its identity through its partner. Now, Scorpio's evolution depends on the fulfillment of the relationship through complete faithfulness.

Fixed emotion is *all out* emotion. Scorps know what they like and what they don't like. Their constancy is admirable and we should not judge them for the extremity of their feelings. They feel strongly and that's why they care so much. Scorpios really don't want you in the foxhole with them if you're going to waver.

Remember, the second sign of Taurus is all about self-worth and resides in the lower half of the zodiac—the "me" side. Directly across from Taurus, on the "we" side, is the sign of Scorpio.

> *Taurus is me and my stuff; Scorpio is we and our stuff.*

With inclusion of the *other* comes vulnerability, the prerequisite for attaining intimacy. Vulnerability implies surrendering to another, which can be terrifying. This is partly why this stage represents the fire that purifies; it strips away defenses. Cinderella can no longer be satisfied with merely attending the ball; now she must "dance with the one who brung her."

Most Scorpios cannot understand that other signs just don't have it in them to be so staunchly devoted. When others don't measure up to their standards, this loyal sign can feel betrayed. Whether those born to this ardent archetype have truly been forsaken or not matters little; it's how they *perceive* the situation. Have a listen to the lyrics of Scorpios Neil Young and Joni Mitchell. The pivotal keyword for Scorpio is *betrayal*. They can feel the cut so deeply that they can become vengeful, for they have so much on the line.

> *The challenge of being a Scorpio is fierce.*
> *Pluto demands that they never betray another.*
> *Scorpionic relationships take place upon an altar of white linen.*

Now, it's easy to see the predicaments in which Libra and Scorpio find themselves. What if their partner changes, no longer feels the same, or leaves? Libra can find itself holding the emotional bag: empty, with an incomplete identity. Scorpio, with its very sense of worth jeopardized, can find it extremely difficult to let go and often tries to manipulate the partner back into their web.

Once a Scorpio man called me to "put me in my place" after I had given a reading to a woman he had dated a few times. She told me how she had just ended their so-called relationship and I was helping her to make sense of why the partnership didn't work out between them. Still busy spinning his web, he said to me, "She *thinks* she's broken up with me."

I cannot tell you how difficult it is for someone who is ending a relationship with another who has strong Scorpio or Plutonian qualities. The other may not even be a Scorpio Sun sign; it can be someone with strong Scorpionic traits in the rest of their natal chart. The willpower emanating from the Scorpion is often experienced as a strong cord of attachment to the soul of another (who usually has weaker willpower). This is clearly related to the Scorpio nature of being "fixed water." Water (emotion) in its fixed state is *ice*. If you ever find yourself in the disfavor of their shadow side, you may feel that they are oblivious to your very *existence*—on purpose. You no longer rate.

When we dig deep (a Scorpio phrase), we find that the key to understanding this sign is the planet Pluto. The farthest of the commonly agreed-upon planets, Pluto is relatively tiny, exceedingly frigid and keeps an eye on the entire solar system. From its distant perch, Pluto rules the sign of Scorpio with a very firm grip. Just as we temper steel, subjecting it to purifying fires, Pluto mercilessly impels us to face our flaws and find the courage to exorcise them. It continually challenges its subjects by questioning *the purity of their own motivations.* Why? To be dedicated, one must be sure of another's intentions.

And this is precisely why they question yours. No wonder they are known for being suspicious; they're suspicious of themselves!

From cold and distant regions
Pluto watches from afar
Hearts cannot escape
This crucible's czar

Shy from its temper of steel
Dare to avoid its black gaze
And keep yourself caged
In a timorous maze

One thing that separates some Scorpio-types from others is the degree to which they project Pluto pressures onto others. What a tortuous world they can end up in if they project their nearly impossible expectations upon others. The tests that go on during this critical phase are, by their very nature, "life or death." Just as an adult accepts the heavy responsibilities of marriage and building a family, this eighth stage starts to take life much more seriously. The bar has suddenly been raised high. We now see the enormity of our incarnation and its significance. From this point on, the zodiacal sojourn is not for the faint of heart.

The definitive question that makes or breaks this archetype is: *how much, if any, self-loathing do they harbor?* The more intolerant they are of themselves, the more intolerant they are of others. How can one filled with self-hatred be otherwise? On the other hand, if they treat themselves with compassion, their soul can radiate a genuinely pure and indomitable character that is rarely equaled, like a precious diamond. If Scorps can harness and channel these turbulent impulses, they can do wonders.

Pluto and Scorpio are representative of the essential principle of "death and rebirth." In their world, the weak must perish. In nature, only the strong survive, and it's Pluto's job to expedite the process of decay so that rebirth may get underway. Someone has to do the dirty work and that job falls on them. Even though this may seem harsh and cold, Pluto and Scorpio do what is necessary for the evolution and survival of the species. They're the undertakers of the zodiac.

The penetrating gaze of the Scorpio artist Pablo Picasso exemplifies this soulfulness. As his artistic vision evolved, he didn't simply change canvasses, he felt compelled to destroy his prior creations. To him, his previous work lacked insight, represented weakness and had to be expunged. This cathartic compulsion is emblematic of the transformative archetype of Scorpio; thus, we see why the zodiac's most resolute sign is the sign of resurrection, the phoenix rising from the ashes. Never count out Scorpio!

Scorpio's realm lies beneath the surface, ruling such things as mining, psychology, death and dying, and the primordial. Nothing escapes their gaze. It is quite common for a Scorpionic person to "look right through you" just as they look right through themselves. With Pluto as their ruler, what else can they do? Impurities do not escape Scorpio's vision. Many people are flat-out uncomfortable in the very presence of a darker Scorpio who doesn't even have to utter a word; their disquieting vibration is simply felt. This is not the place to even think about hiding your agenda. If you don't intend to take the game seriously, *then don't play;* that's Scorpio.

We can see how the relationship signs hold many perplexing conundrums. Libra's is that while the Scales want to remain balanced, they can become paralyzed, unable to lean far in either direction. Scorpio's is that to achieve the intimacy they desire, the openness they fear is a prerequisite. Yet, vulnerability threatens their very security, which can mire this sign in a lose-lose situation. On the other hand, the shadow side of this archetype can be quite pitiless toward themselves and others: "You've made your bed, now lie in it!" Successful Scorpios can resolve this dilemma by showing more self-compassion.

Evolving man is not only toughening up but is now ready to wield its power. Scorpio is getting smarter. Knowledge is power and *power* is Scorpio's middle name. Whether it is used to dominate others or for a higher purpose is largely up to them. It is not uncommon for those with charts permeated with the Scorpio archetype to be predisposed to relationships in which power is not equally shared. The pure passion of Scorpion energies can easily lead to domination over the other.

Dominating or being dominated are both indicators of low-esteem.

The act of surrendering the self opens the door to true relationships; unhealthy codependency and submission/domination can only be avoided if each partner has a strong sense of self. "Getting lost in another" is part and parcel of falling in love but not to the point where one usurps the other's psyche. Remember, Scorpio's opposite sign of Taurus is strongly attached to what they *have.* In the "we" half of the zodiac, Scorpio can become totally preoccupied with *owning* their partner—a perilous obsession. This explains why they are frequently paranoid, possessive and jealous and can use sexual manipulation towards this end. It's often a battle of wills.

No sign has willpower that even comes close to matching Scorpio's. Because of their fixed nature, it's very difficult for them to relinquish a relationship that is dying. On the plus side, Scorpios are one hundred percent dedicated to those they love; they will accept nothing less from themselves.

Those with strong Pluto/Scorpio traits in their charts can barely contain their penetrating gaze. What they love, they idolize; what they hate, they despise. There is no middle ground. Therefore, we see an intrinsic difficulty with this stage of the zodiac. With a tendency towards such dramatically polarized feelings, it is challenging to remain in touch with life's subtleties and lightness. In this way, Scorpio shares characteristics with the sign Virgo. Virgo separates the wheat from the chaff but Scorpio judges whether or not an object even has a right to exist! To Virgo, weakness is to be frowned upon but tolerated; to Scorpio, it is to be destroyed, perhaps even turned to ashes. Both signs share an unequivocal purity of purpose. Scorpio is adamant about their purity of intention and convictions from which their beauty and courage emanate.

I have found that those with a preponderance of Scorpio markers in their chart find it difficult to overcome their shadow side. Conversely, many a weaker Sun sign can have their birth chart totally altered, if not salvaged, with a dose of Scorpio or Pluto energy. Some charts need that added oomph.

Many Scorps represent the impeccable side of the human race. Known for their courage, they can achieve great heights: General George Patton, President Theodore Roosevelt, Madame Curie, Walter Cronkite, Dr. Jonas Salk, Bill Gates, Will Rogers, Rev. Billy Graham, Indira Gandhi and Robert Kennedy. Talk about responsibility; Scorpio shoulders life's burdens like few others. Don't tell them to lighten up, back off or let it slide. That's just not in their nature.

In the signs of Libra and Scorpio, man has been tested in his ability to relate to others. Whether this growing entity has become consumed by self-loathing or has learned self-forgiveness is the crux of the matter. Only when one's inner demons have been conquered can that person join with another in a healthy fashion. Successful completion of this stage is crucial to the progress of the developing self. Having survived this acid test, evolving man is stronger, more resilient and self-possessed. Now, we prepare ourselves for a broader experience.

Intimacy is possible because of Scorpio; integrity finds us and, as a result, our arrow's aim is truer. Great reverence is reserved for the integrity of this unwavering sign. For the final time, we rise from the ashes and bank toward the unbounded skies of Sagittarius.

"Confession is always weakness.
The grave soul keeps its own secrets,
and takes its own punishment in silence."

—*Dorothy Dix*

Sagittarius: Between a Rock and a Hot Place

The Archer's high trajectory transcends the emotional sweat lodge of Scorpio, where we surely paid our dues. Sagittarius, the last sign of the relationship quadrant, has graduated from personal relationships and now sets its sights on camaraderie. It extends its reach and joins hands with those around the world. The prolonged pain of purification during the Scorpio experience results in this fire sign, Sagittarius, wanting to have fun and not take life so seriously.

This free-spirited sign presents us with a dramatic change from Scorpio. These natives are optimistic, carefree and expressive. They absolutely abhor downbeats and suppression of any kind. Thus, they are commonly known for being blunt and outspoken. Their strong need for honesty sometimes leads them to behave as if "the end justifies the means" and not always with the desired results. Sometimes, this not only finds them with both shoes firmly planted in their mouths, it can get them into loads of mischief, as well. This sign, along with Gemini and Pisces, knows little of self-discipline: the beauty of Sag is its unfettered *enthusiasm*.

Most people love being around fun-loving Sagittarians, personified by celebrities such as Bette Midler, Jon Stewart and Ben Stiller. Their enthusiasm is simply contagious. The epitome of Sagittarians, Walt Disney reached out to all people. Representing the idealistic Archer, his broad vision of the world was unparalleled. He invited all to come and have fun! His image is permanently etched in our minds: arms outstretched in front of his Magic Kingdom, sparking our imagination with cascading fireworks. He exemplified the archetypal essence of this "mutable fire" sign.

The Archer's motto is, "If it isn't fun, I'm just not going to do it!" This devil-may-care attitude can verge on flippancy. It's simply not in their nature to burden themselves in any way. This is an all-too-common characteristic of this sign. Quite capricious, the fun one often wonders, "Why can't other signs simply chill out? Why do they have to take everything so seriously?"

Take the example of a balloon, a colorful symbol of gaiety. Now, equate Scorpio with the growing intensity of air pressure in the expanding balloon, and Sagittarius with the release that takes place as the balloon pops or ricochets wildly around the room. It's not intended for a destination.

Like a bat out of hell, Sagittarius just wants
to escape the heat of Scorpio's kitchen.

Sag has the least down side of any of the zodiacal dozen. Known for being lucky, they commonly come away from trouble unscathed, always landing on their feet. Certainly Bugs Bunny was the epitome of this type of footloose, freewheeling energy. "What's up, Doc?" What's up is that this big-mouthed, irreverent prankster gets away with just about anything.

Sag has to expand its stomping grounds; they have to move on, as with all the fire signs. Physically active, most of them love the outdoors and many have a special fondness for horses. The Centaur's dual symbolism represents the lower half of the untamed wild horse, as well as the higher dimension Sagittarians who are idealistic and aspiring. It's no wonder why Sagittarius rules the upper legs and thighs, as these are the largest and most powerful muscles that thrust our bodies forward.

To Sag, "it's all good!" Because of their bubbly, outgoing nature, they are the salesmen of the zodiac, as well as the clowns: Harpo Marx, Woody Allen, Ray Romano, Steve Buscemi and Richard Pryor. They're naturals when it comes to humor. This ninth sign is gung-ho about having a good time. A great many of them say the word "fun" in every third or fourth sentence—and why not? Caught between a rock (Capricorn) and a hot place (Scorpio), this happy harlequin reaches for new heights as it unconsciously prepares the way for the Goat to ascend the mountain regions of the zodiac and the summit of Mt. Capricorn.

American astrologer Stephen Arroyo calls Sagittarius "the source of self-confidence." How apropos. When we encounter the Sagittarian ruling planet, Jupiter, we often sense a swelling of our self-worth, a feeling of assuredness and an overall air of well being and lightness. Socialite Jupiter gives us great confidence as we mix with others. (You only have to stare in wonder at how Jupiter's brilliance outshines all other stars in the night sky in order to get a sense of this confidence.) The solar system's largest planet brings us benevolence and cheer. Sag/Jupiter is that burgeoning *knowing* that we get just before we roll a seven in Vegas. It's that irrepressible energy that we conjure when we do the wave at the stadium; it's a rally cap. It's the natural, ebullient, childlike faith we have in life itself, a *positive attitude*.

However, Sag's bed of roses can also be thorny. For some reason, similar to Gemini, Sag likes to poke fun at others and sometimes their verbal barbs can penetrate deeply. Both archetypes can objectify others and then backpedal, insisting that no harm was intended. Many times, though, harm *was* done. Just like its opposite sign of Gemini, Sag has a dual (although not as polarized) nature. Both signs are often uneasy when held accountable for their actions; however, fire is *spirit*, and true spirit usually acts without malice. Fire not only warms, it can singe.

Sag sees their straightforwardness as acceptable, even laudable, for they can't stand dishonesty in any way. This sign is going to let you know how they feel, period. They can't keep their "truth" pent up; it will seep out of their pores somehow. Sagittarius can really use a touch of milder astrological energies to give them some much needed tact. A hearty slap on the back doesn't always make it better.

Some things, once said, can never be taken back.

The change that takes place from Scorpio to Sagittarius mirrors the transition that took place from Taurus to Gemini. You'll recall how growing man was somewhat stuck in the status quo and stagnancy of Taurus and then found flight in the sign of Gemini. In a very similar fashion, Sagittarius simply must transcend the melodramatic emotion of Scorpio in exchange for clear, unbounded skies. Next, just as Gemini plunges hard into the watery seas of Cancer, Sagittarius smacks into Capricorn's earthen walls. Notice another interesting parallel with the Archer's opposing sign of Gemini: the Twins evade taking positions on just about everything, while

Sag evades the intimacy that was so hard won in Scorpio! The closeness that was once relentlessly pursued may now be experienced as suffocating, and Sag can't stand being stifled. In fact, no sign suffers more from cabin fever. Gemini and Sag must be free to roam.

It is always important to draw the ✗ glyph of the Archer with its arrow pointing upward. Sag is upbeat, light and open—unlike the dark, mysterious Scorpio who dwells deep in murky waters, ever vigilant about revealing itself. Hasn't the "self" been cooked enough in the sign of Scorpio? "Most certainly!" says Sag. This strange bedfellow is interjected just before the disciplinarian Capricorn, the most stoic of all the twelve signs. Sag lets it all hang out, and this leads the Centaur to its potential pitfall. They mean well with their enthusiastic spirit; for example, they eagerly volunteer for anything that sounds like fun but once they learn how much heavy lifting is involved, they tend to split. When it comes to accepting personal consequences, they tend to waffle. Consistently, we have seen evolving man take on more and more responsibility yet this loosey-goosey sign often recoils from accountability. This is exactly why they have the reputation for promising and not delivering.

The myth of Sagittarius is that if they laugh it off, all will be okay.

I have an indelible vision of this carefree sign: a van with its doors wide open. "Come on, get in! Bring your friends! The more the merrier!" Many times, this gets them into a truckload of shenanigans, too. Excess and waste are common after-effects that are associated with this sign. *Pre-Saturnian* Sagittarius knows no limits, as it has not yet bowed to the jurisdiction of Saturn and its frozen rings of containment.

Exactly why is this Centaur so high-spirited and restless? Is it because they sense winter coming? I have had many Sag clients tell me, "I love to travel. I'll go anywhere. I just want to go somewhere." (What they really want is to escape the inner inquisition of Scorpio.) Many Sagittarians simply can't wrap their heads around the idea of working nine to five in a dreary, stuffy office. In fact, those with an excessive Sagittarian stamp really feel restricted in conventional relationships, which they find unnecessarily limiting. Why can't they enjoy a second person or a third? It's fun! Taking responsibility for their infidelities . . . well, that's another story.

Unfortunately and mistakenly, too many times Sag is simply looked at as the court jester, when they have much more to offer. Most are voracious readers and perennial students. They usually have a hard time deciding on their major field of study because they are interested in so many different fields; how can they choose just one? It is not their nature to limit themselves.

The college experience itself is Sagittarian.

Further observation shows us just how Sagittarius and Capricorn, ruled by Jupiter and Saturn, respectively, tell us much about our social sensibilities. Sagittarius chafes at social restrictions, even though it ironically rules governments and codes of ethics. Sagittarians are often found proselytizing to others but don't always walk their walk. They often provide too much information! Show me someone with a great interest in politics or government and usually you'll find a strong theme of the Jupiter/Sagittarian makeup in their natal chart. Even though they are the zodiac's most politically oriented sign, the advancing self doesn't accept this conformity until the next sign of Capricorn.

Why does Sag's visionary arrow tilt upward? It's telling mankind, "We can make it to the top! We can do this!" Sag is the cheerleader of the zodiac. It's the energy we summon from within when we need to give ourselves a pep talk. This uplifting archetype appears at critical junctures: Sagittarian Winston Churchill's words of encouragement had an overwhelmingly heartening effect upon the British during World War II. I'm sure that the Chileans caught in the 2010 mine collapse exemplified this Jovian (Jupiterian) archetype. By keeping their morale high and their sense of humor intact, they greatly increased their odds for a successful rescue.

Sagittarian's vista is global and rules a wide field of activities: education, government, law, travel, broadcasting, and political and social causes. Sag is one big sign, just as Jupiter is the solar system's largest planet.

Jupiter just smiles
At life's broken toys
Its humor restores
With faith and with joy

It wears its red spot
Like a dimple not a scar
A playful reminder
That to the planets, it's a star

"Big" doesn't always mean "better," however. It is clear that all three fire signs can have quite a reputation for exaggeration. One of Sag's shadow traits is disingenuousness. Due to their zeal, they can get caught up in the spirit of the moment and are left defending their own confabulation. These tendencies come from avoiding life's intricacies, which can also cause them to gloss over life's nuances; they paint life in broad strokes. Sagittarius often goes off half-cocked, not equipped with all the facts. The opposite side of the zodiac holds their answer: Gemini and its informed, factual nature. Self-fascination comes with the sign of the Twins, who are so intrigued with how the mind works. In its reflective half, Sagittarius is enthralled with how *all* of our minds work, our beliefs and overall philosophies.

As you may have guessed by now, Sagittarius can be confounding. Why do both Gemini and Sagittarius tend to have biting tongues? Like Hendrix's big bang guitar riffs that explode and then dissipate into vapor trails, Sag expounds its social truths and ethics but finds it hard to track their own arrows. Jim Morrison often showed up late and inebriated for performances with *The Doors*.

We've come all the way to the ninth stage of the zodiac and yet we find this larger-than-life sign recklessly scrambling out from between a rock and a hot place. Is Sag just looking to escape its duties? How could his all have come about at this rather "advanced" stage of man's evolution?

It had to happen. It's all part of the zodiac's exquisite intelligence.

Sagittarius is the buffer between Scorpio and Capricorn. One of the twelve signs *has* to express life's vastness and Sag can't do so with the heavy obligations that belong to each of its neighbors. Sag is not meant to be a constant flame; its job, like a sparkler, is to excite.

How could it be possible to go from Scorpio to Capricorn
without letting off some steam, some comic relief?

Along the creative path, to indulge or analyze kills the creative flow. Our accomplishments matter far less than the *spirit* of the effort. Are we enjoying the journey? Are we having fun? Sagittarians teach us this. We're captives of the past until the joker's magic breaks the spell. Through humor and release we shatter old conceptual frameworks, replacing them with ones that are more robust and beyond our wildest dreams.

The ninth stage of the zodiac is not the place for rules and consistency. It's much more important now that man foregoes the old worn path in order to explore new territory. It's time for Sag to fuel its fire without considering the aftermath. How could this sign deliver on all of its promises without cramping its style? It simply can't be done.

As mentioned already, no sign can do it all. The zodiac weaves its way through a perfect circle, not a straight line. When we graduate from Scorpio, we stop fixating on the self, and in the vivacious sign of Sagittarius, intolerance comes to an end. With the loss of self-absorption, intolerance of others disappears, for what is intolerance other than projection? Sag is big and it takes on a lot; it takes on the whole world, literally. It is consumed with fire and re-enthuses all of us for the final ascent to the summit. Consistency is saved for the tough old Goat coming next. The Archer means well because it epitomizes optimism—and without this spirit for life, we'd all curl up and die.

Because of this explorer emeritus, our world has become unimaginably vast and vital. Because we are now educated and our associations now extend beyond our immediate circle, we have each become bigger. The transition has taken place from the personal to the social to the collective.

With Sag, the section of the zodiac pertaining to relationships is now concluded and we are ready to enter the final quadrant, where our intentions reach to the edges of the world and beyond, and where the collective lives.

Because of this iridescent fire sign, evolving man has wandered off and found himself matriculating at the school of life. He is now poised to secure a prestigious social position in the sign of Capricorn. Thanks to hopeful, jubilant Sagittarius, we have regained our momentum.

Many years ago, my extended family and I were enjoying a picnic together. In the cool of the evening, we started to capture lightning bugs in glass jars that had holes punched into their metal lids. Excitedly, I ran up a nearby hill with my three-year-old nephew. I was panting and he was having a blast. We paused under a tree at the top of the hill and had a Sag moment.

"Uncle Rick!" he exclaimed.

"Yes," I replied.

Having fun and not even knowing why, he whispered quietly to me: "What are we doin?"

Capricorn: Are You Sure?

Find a decent job and work hard, get married and have 2.1 children, buy a beautiful home in a safe neighborhood, drive your SUV with side air bags, color insides the lines at all times . . . and you'll be okay.

That's the Capricorn myth. As we continue our sojourn through the "other-oriented" half of the astrological wheel, we arrive at the zenith of the zodiac, the first stage that willingly sacrifices itself for the whole.

This sign sits on top symbolizing the pinnacle of social hierarchy. Former heavyweight boxer Mohammed Ali used to boast, "I am the greatest!" Known not only for his pugilistic prowess, he was also regarded for using his Capricornian command, power and prestige to influence humanitarian causes. The pure archetype underlying this sign is entrusted with this principal position because it's now willing to take on the responsibilities that come with the territory. Think of Martin Luther King, Ben Franklin, Edgar Allen Poe, Denzel Washington, J. R. R. Tolkein, Michelle Obama, Stephen Hawking and Kahlil Gibran.

A very ambitious sign, it claims the head seat at the corporate board meeting and has the traditional gold name plate on the front of the desk. They take their station seriously (and just about everything else, too). Even so, Capricorn probably has one of the worst reputations in the zodiac because they're thought of as being rigid and pessimistic. Much of this is ill-founded and certainly not deserved because this sign voluntarily takes on the weight of the world.

At the pure archetypal level, the final signs are the epitome of being truly "other-oriented." This last quadrant is purely about the "collective mind"—the minds and hearts of all of us combined. When it comes to the stages of man, these are the "elders." Capricornian, Aquarian and Piscean babies often seem like old souls. Universal consciousness is broadest in this concluding quadrant.

Due to their adverse reaction to the carelessness of Sagittarius, Capricorn is imbued with a great sense of stewardship and attentiveness. Sagittarius made the mess and Capricorn comes in to clean it up. Being an earth sign makes this archetype quite practical, and belonging to the cardinal mode invests them with the thrust of natural-born leaders. They are probably the most conventional and pragmatic of all the twelve; the model they provide is a prudent one. Many obstacles had to be overcome during the previous nine developmental stages of cosmic man in order for us to emerge here at the summit.

Duty and responsibility are deeply embedded Capricorn characteristics. There's no reason to question the acceptance of consequences here; responsibility is Capricorn's middle name (maybe even its first). Social position is everything to this respectful archetype. Keeping the opposite sign in mind, remember that Cancer makes its home within the nuclear family; with Capricorn, it's about the "family of man."

In its natural state, the mountain goat must be cautious and watch each step. The Goat is a sure-footed animal but surprisingly flirts with disaster, treading close to the edge. (Look at the life of President Richard Nixon as an example of how far some can fall.)

Capricorn is the initial sign of the last quadrant, the quarter of the zodiac pertaining to *the collective, or the world and beyond*. In this pivotal stage, the wise old man gains the title of emeritus. And the best way to achieve and preserve this stature (at least he thinks so) is to do what he is *supposed* to do: follow the rules. Very similar to the sign of Virgo, Capricorn behaves in an obeisant manner while Virgo does what is *right*—there is a difference. Capricorn does what is best to comply with the accepted social norms and is always keenly sensitive to the social barometer.

The tried and true is the path of the Goat; leave the wild adventuring and pioneering to Aries, Sag and Aquarius. The careful, step-by-step gait is what allows Capricorn to consistently climb the corporate ladder; they know how to play the game. Don't challenge this sign to a game of paintball; they play strategically and know how to use nearby structures in their environment to their advantage. They don't take risks; however, Capricorn often falls short when they have to improvise or think outside the box. Many Goats fall flat on their beards. It is often painful to watch a Capricorn waiver when they learn that they are free to do what they want. Some birds won't leave their cages even though the door has been left wide open. More than a few Caps have no idea how to be spontaneous. (Ironically, these effervescent qualities were just hard won in Sagittarius.) Capricorn often settles for less in life because they play it too safe. The Capricorn makeup is ill at ease with jazzy, impromptu improvisations. Just picture a monocled British businessman corkscrewing his moustache and saying, "Why, that Sagittarian chap is simply out of control!"

At this critical evolutionary moment, the entity starts to address needs beyond its comfort zone. For the gears of any social machine to turn smoothly and run effectively, all of the cogs must be perfectly calibrated. That's why things run like clockwork with Capricorn; the zodiac's Father sees the bigger picture. Capricorns *attune to the needs of the society* as they heroically sacrifice their individuality for a higher cause (and hardly ever get any credit). Ironically, we find that aristocratic Capricorn is a well-meaning Socialist. What a predicament!

Nevertheless, Capricorn is vigilant about the functioning of society as a whole; thus, the tendency towards regulation. Traffic lights must have been invented by a Capricorn; we can't all have a green light at the same time, can we, Aries? Many goats are appropriately cast as ultra-conservative, overly traditional and even stoical; therefore, they give great effort to adhering to social norms and are adamant about being seen as inculpable and innocent.

Capricorns try so hard to do things "properly."

Well then, just what is "proper" other than an agreed upon set of standards? In reality, there are no standards by which to live yet behaving properly is inherent to the archetype of Capricorn. (Put that in your government-issued pipe and try to light it!) All consensus standards are malleable and are coined by an ever-changing larger whole. I recall many times asking my Italian immigrant father, a Capricorn himself, "Dad, how do you want to do this?" He'd always reply with his thick accent, "How you spose ta do it?"

The odds of being so punctilious increase if the person's chart has multiple planets in Capricorn or major planetary aspects to Saturn. Capricorn is the disciplinarian as well as the judge. The most common planetary placement I see in the charts of successful people is a strategically placed Saturn. Why is this so? Because you aren't going to get far in life unless you have some type of self-command, some stick-to-it-ness. Many times, the reason why a Saturnine personality succeeds is that the ringed mammoth is such a pain in the posterior that it simply frustrates us into action.

Saturn frets and worries
So the others can be
However they choose
To see what they see

Now, does not the mother
Get the credit for cheer
While the father makes sure
That the child knows no fear?

The Capricornian constitution is founded on two simple words: make sure. What was once just a thought is brought into form in the sign of Capricorn. It is their sole duty to materialize, crystallize and consolidate whatever they touch.

When you need a job to get done, give it to a Capricorn.

Caps will deliver the goods, as they are heads and tails above any other sign when it comes to dependability. Granted, Virgos may be the most efficient and capable but Capricorn will stay up all night, sweating profusely to make *sure* that the project gets completed. Therein lies the rub. Many call Saturn the taskmaster but Saturn doesn't tie us up with chains and handcuffs; it does so with *fear*. Fear of what? Fear of a task falling through the cracks or being done haphazardly. When the Capricornian brickmaker has made his brick perfectly to standard, the time has come to let it dry. No more sweating and fussing will help. That is the very challenge for this mountain climber: *trusting and letting go.*

The natural inclination of a Goat, raised amidst the crags of a mountain peak, is to *not* let go.

Another common issue for the Capricorn and Saturnian archetypes is what to do when a fork is encountered in the road. Let's say the Goat starts down the left path. It is all too common for this archetype to sweat each step taken because, if he is wrong, look how far he has to backtrack to get on the "right" path. It would be the same, of course, if he had first chosen the fork to the right. This stymies many Goats at the onset of their journey, before they can even get on track. To their dismay, there just aren't any guarantees.

Quite commonly, Capricorns freeze at this point and become paralyzed.

Saturnian issues are among the most immobilizing and life-challenging in astrology. Why? Because of fear of the unknown. Most of us are uncomfortable with uncertainty but in a larger context, control is a myth and taking risks is unavoidable. There is a great misunderstanding about Capricorn and Saturn: Capricorn isn't obsessed about being in control; rather, it has a great fear of situations getting out of hand. There's a difference.

You can't control life's stream. Surely, you can try to influence its direction but you cannot take definitive charge over every droplet of water. It is absolutely impossible to guarantee the path that your life will take. The answer to Saturnian problems is to do your best to flow with the current and guide your boat's general direction. *That* is within your purview and will greatly decrease your stress level. Before you know it, you will have probably arrived at your destination all in one piece, safe and sound. I always tell Capricorns:

Be careful to not be too careful.

Capricorn clients often ask me *how* to go with the flow. I tell them, "If you have to ask, you're not going with the flow." When I tell them that there is no "how to" manual for life, I really don't think they believe me! Going with the flow is diametrically opposed to Saturn/Capricorn's nature. The Goat's gingerly way of moving even applies to children. Capricornian children are known for being well behaved and instinctively following rules. They are a serious lot well before their first birthday. As they grow older, they start to rebel against their own worrisome nature and many of them tend to loosen up as they age.

Many times when we ask our elders what they might have done differently if they could turn back the hands of time, they say, "I wouldn't have been so cautious," or "I would have taken more risks." These regrets are all too common when we allow Saturn (Capricorn's ruling planet) to wrap its icy rings around us too tightly.

This cautious tendency toward conformity and conventionality can often bring about perfunctory, hollow relationships. Yes, married people are supposed to "honor and obey" but you can do all the things that a spouse should do and still not have marital bliss. Many a Cap find themselves in distress later in life if they have not developed flexibility along the way and have ignored their inner promptings. Just because they have up-to-date memberships at the country club and are listed in *Who's Who* matters little in the overall scheme of things. Individuality is sacrificed when one conforms to the macrocosm.

Just as the *family* is everything to the Cancerian archetype, Capricorn's central need is also to *belong*; this emotionally challenged sign needs its nest, too, only this time it's their corner office and not necessarily the family unit.

No sign feels the pain of ostracism from the tribe more than Capricorn.

Each zodiacal stage has its imperative: to complete the next level of growth according to the cosmic blueprint. Because of this rugged sign, we are granted stamina and a sense of behaving, or what The Buddha called *right* action in his teachings of the Noble Eightfold Path. This responsible way of being is necessary, not a penance. It may sound old-fashioned in these modern times but one could call Capricorns model citizens. (Decency is a quality that is sorely missing in today's world.) That's the Capricorn archetype, the Hierophant (the rigid dogmatic judge) of the Tarot deck. Do you see why the wary Cancer archetype is traditionally paired up with this prudent patriarchal sign?

So, that is Capricorn: the cranky, conservative, careful cuss. Other signs have more flair and daring. Other signs may be smarter and warmer and more energetic but no sign is more dependable and reliable, or takes you as seriously as you take yourself. Capricorn is respectful and reverent. There is an innate grandeur about their stately manner. Sir Frodo Baggins of The *Lord of the Rings* was entrusted to carry the ring because he was the perfect archetype of Capricorn.

There is a beauty to Capricorn's allegiance and sense of duty, too. They are willing to sacrifice themselves for the good of the rest of us wayward souls. The Goat is constantly underestimated because it's so low key. Plenty of Caps have an earthy and dry sense of humor: Jim Carrey, Betty White and Andy Rooney; however, Capricorn doesn't take life for granted. It was fun and games in the sign of Sagittarius but things have changed; now, its focus is on how we all live together. Its nature is to establish institutions and social structures that serve mankind. It prepares the soul for liftoff in the final two stages.

When you're in real trouble and you need someone to come through for you and bail you out, where do you go? You go to the venerated Godfather: Capricorn. So, what has it gotten the Goat who is now seated on the throne of the zodiac? He is at the top yet the roughest terrain and greatest challenges still lie ahead, as with the Hobbits on Mt. Doom. Even so, this triumph is only fleeting, like all victories. Being on top is just another moment. It was an illusion all along that lured us to the pinnacle; it was the Sagittarian *quest for the apogee itself* that held the intrigue. Once again, we prove that it's the journey that really matters, not the destination. If the mastery of this stage is not put into proper perspective but instead mistakenly seen as the ultimate goal itself, it would be all downhill from here, would it not? The ego cannot afford to fall from such a height.

What are we really discovering once we open the door to the world beyond? There is only a split second when we are at the very top of the wheel, the moment when the noble Archer genuflects and passes its torch to Capricorn. During that moment, fire touches earth for the last time and infuses Mother Gaia with the *Holy Spirit*.

At this point, our climb is over.

In that fraction of a second, evolving man takes his focus and shifts from the self to the All. What a big change, indeed. Capricorn can relish its time on top, if it wishes but why doesn't the zodiac end here? The answer is that the top of the world is not really the goal. Your Gold Card is no good in heaven.

The seat at the apex of the zodiacal wheel is a very special point of culmination for each of us but it must be relinquished because that's the nature of this game. Our individual achievements can only take us so high. On its way back down, as you will see in the next chapter, Aquarius claims the bounty for all. There comes a time when the horn of plenty must be shared in Aquarius and ultimately sacrificed in Pisces. We have two more rounds to go in this exquisite wheel.

Aquarius: Enigma and Anomaly

"You blew it!" says the eleventh sign of Aquarius to its predecessor.

"What do you mean?" Capricorn replies.

"You had it made," Aquarius explains. "You were on top of the world. You had achieved everything but you conformed to such a degree that you lost your very identity. You blew it!"

Thus we begin the sign of Aquarius with its major emphasis on restoring and furthering our sense of uniqueness. Aquarius stands atop the successful shoulders of Capricorn. From this lofty position, the Water Bearer is able to view the broad vista of life, the highest dimension of the mind. Capricorn needed to adhere to social structures in order to establish and advance itself. Now, Aquarius realizes that to attain the summit while having disowned the self yields quite an empty victory, indeed.

Individual and equal rights are essential to Aquarians. It's obvious to see that Capricorn's need for the conventional is in direct contrast to the Aquarian need for the unconventional—"inside the box" versus "outside the box." Autonomy and innovative thinking are Aquarius' comfort zone. This is the sign of the inventor, the genius, the true visionary. Aquarians are, as a rule, decades ahead of their time: Thomas Edison, Federico Fellini, Jack Nicklaus, Wolfgang Mozart, FDR, James Joyce, Helen Gurley Brown, Jackie Robinson, Oprah Winfrey, and also Abraham Lincoln and Charles Darwin, who were born on the same day and year.

Like a thunderbolt, the Aquarian archetype explodes out of the status quo of Capricorn and shockingly gives us new freedom and higher insights. As father time (Saturn) catches up with all things, what was once Aquarian or new will eventually stagnate and grow old. With a Uranian renewal (the planetary ruler of Aquarius,) we start the cycle all over again. This dance of old-new-old-new goes on endlessly.

In my astrology practice, the most common ailment amongst my clients is that they hang onto their old habits and behavior patterns even when they have become outdated, ineffective and even toxic. Capricorn/ Saturn coalesces and consolidates. Aquarius breaks the stalemate of the status quo and takes us to the next cutting edge; thus, the Aquarian reputation for being the radical and the rebel. The Water Bearer splashes water in our faces to awaken us.

Gemini, the first air sign, explores the possibility of thought and communication, as well as how the mind works. Libra, the second air sign, is keenly attuned to social thinking. Now in our final air sign, Aquarius reaches for the highest dimension of thought: the vast perplexing states of paradox itself, the domain of contradictions and polarities. Aquarius – Contrarius. Ruled by the planet Uranus and co-ruled by Saturn, Aquarius is a recalcitrant archetype, very unpredictable. One cannot have free will yet remain predictable. It is up to the individual whether their degree of contrariness results in a disruptive, disagreeable demeanor or blesses them with a healthy, tolerant perspective on life. If a person exhibits qualities such as genius, inventiveness, great self-independence and common flashes of brilliance, they certainly have strong Aquarian traits in their chart or key aspects to the planet Uranus.

This strange bird of Uranus
Rolls on its side and has us perplexed
What's up and what's down
What's bygone and what's next

Its largesse is quite broad
Connecting all that we see
Often stumbling alone
Not fusing, not free

Let's zoom in closer to pin down the source from where these Aquarian traits of future vision and idealism originate. Aquarius is a "fixed air" sign, meaning that those with this archetype in their charts have highly concentrated minds. They organize their thoughts into one huge correlated mental matrix. This is why they constantly are on the lookout for opposite extremes and apparent contradictions. In this way, they broaden their world of perception and include all ideas.

Nothing is verboten to Aquarius. Above all, they seek the *ramifications of any two ideas.*

> *Given this and given that, Aquarius says,*
> *"Do you realize what that means?"*

Whether it's solving a riddle or contemplating the koan about the sound of one hand clapping, Aquarius lives at the apparent contradiction. Wisdom consistently reveals how two extremes are not opposites but two sides of the same coin. While most of us are imprisoned within our own imaginary quagmires, contrasting between this *or* that, Aquarius naturally resolves conflicts by consolidating both this *and* that. By way of example, a knife is quite an essential instrument used during surgery, and that very same knife is not what you want to see wielded against you in a dark alley.

Welcome to the land of the higher mind—Aquarius—where polarities start to blend in order for all of us to see the bigger picture—thus, the maddening-liberating state of the Water Bearer. (It's actually an air sign even though it has "aqua" in its name.) They are friendly but aloof, conservative yet liberal, broad minded yet mentally rigid (fixed). They want a relationship but fear for their freedom. It is commonly said of this sign that "they love mankind; it's people they can't stand."

This archetypal domain is laden with conundrums and transgressions against the norm. Why is this so? Their need is to expand beyond the three-dimensional, Newtonian world of duality and predictability—theirs is the perplexing, irrational realm of Heisenberg and quantum mechanics—where one thing *can* be in two places at once. Alice surely found Aquarian terrain when she discovered *Wonderland* through the rabbit hole.

If Capricorn can be symbolized by a skyscraper, then Aquarius is best matched to a geodesic dome. Instead of a monolith towering above the "commoners," the dome is made up of all equal parts and offers collective strength. Its inherent shape provides a broader shelter as stresses are shouldered equally.

Aquarius brings us a broader home than Cancer did earlier; it is the domain of all nations. To Aquarius, there is no limited horizon. They treat their children more like friends than possessions or ego-extensions. Equality is a given, not a goal. The Water Bearer generously spreads its life-giving elixir liberally to all the world.

"Groupthink" . . . that's Aquarius.

Imbued with scholarly obsessions, their great preoccupation is to research and unify the giant mental puzzle. (Yes, Albert Einstein's chart was dominated by the planet Uranus.) They have a pure attraction to and quest for ideas and ideals—the beauty and symmetry of cerebral cohesion. Continuing the theme of sacrifice, which began in Capricorn, Aquarius goes one better. Because of their love of humanity and the earth, they are by extension concerned about all things environmental. These natives have been collectively drumming their fingers for more than forty years waiting for the rest of us to finally address alternative energy sources. They can be found getting involved in grassroots campaigns, collective efforts and think tanks. They invented Sci-Fi (Jules Verne was Aquarian) and envisioned space travel before Sputnik; they long ago tired of warring as they dreamt of utopia—a theme that many of us sadly label as naïve or Pollyannaish.

Aquarians want to keep us from blowing up our only planet!

Since they are no longer plagued by interpersonal issues (relatively speaking), the Aquarian archetype does not need the assent or blessings of others. Their constitution is mentally and emotionally self-sufficient. This allows them to appreciate uniqueness in others and engenders the tolerance they have for all people.

Although Piscean, the late Fred Rogers of TV's *Mr. Rogers' Neighborhood* gave such a consistent Uranian message to our young and old alike: "You are special and there is no one like you!" This genteel and quiet-spoken man may have sounded corny to some but the impact of his Aquarian message still resonates across the generations. The basic precepts of the world's great religions are that we get along, not judge each other, and have tolerance and treat our neighbors as ourselves. These are all major Aquarian tenets. And if our iconic Statue of Liberty symbolizes any sign, it's Aquarius. Man's focus is now eclipsing individual needs. This is *the* sign that is the advocate for planet earth and all of its residents.

This complicated sign is consistently taken for granted. A remarkable quality about Aquarians is their unconditional loyalty to others. We commonly lament just how hard it is to find a loyal friend. Theirs is the sign of *true* friendship, a term we glibly toss about. On the archetypal level, one way of putting it is that the preceding ten stages have had strings attached to their motivations. Aquarians are not looking for something in exchange for their allegiance other than friendship.

The Water Bearer's fondness of camaraderie is not like Cancer, who absorbs the warmth and comfort of the group; nor is it like the confirmation of one's identity sought by Librans and Capricorns. Aquarius is the group. It is the common heartbeat. The relative stage of the soul has made a quantum leap in this penultimate sign, the highest potential of *individuality as a self.*

It's quite Aquarian to hang out with people of varying ages. Younger or older, this sign sees the humanity in everyone and revels in the diversity across all cultures, races, ages and genders. They see other people as their brothers and sisters across this beautiful blue orb. While receiving respect is paramount for the sign of Leo, in this opposite sign of Aquarius, respect is something to be extended to all.

This is not to say, of course, that every Aquarian is a perfect model citizen. Their life-giving waters can sometimes become brackish. A shadow side of this sign is the "rebel without a cause" (James Dean, Ayn Rand, Angela Davis, Governor Sarah Palin and Glenn Beck, are Aquarians). Their oftentimes stubborn mindset is the flip side of a self-assured intellect, and can become quite self-serving and dangerous. If not careful, Aquarius can end up in a warped house of mirrors from attempting to make the world in their own image. They can ride roughshod over other people's sensibilities with their fanatical beliefs. Other capricious Aquarians can become disruptive just to shake up the powers that be, or just to be different. The myth of this eleventh sign is that they'll come out okay if they do everything their own way. But, they simply cannot be unconventional *all the time.* No man is an island.

They have a great fear of being weighed down by others' emotional baggage and have little time for the games people play. Frequently, due to their independence and emotional detachment, they are labeled as cold and aloof. Even though emotional distance can cause great loneliness, Aquarians, more than any other sign, do very well living by themselves.

Aquarians love to leave.

I know that seems like a strange thought. Because of their strong need for independence and fear of being corralled, I've often found it amusing to observe how quickly Aquarians leave the room, leave a group, leave a relationship. It's quite a natural response for them to just pack up and split.

I recently met with an Aquarian couple who are clients of mine. To their great fortune, they have both discovered (after having had years of unrewarding relationships) that to truly surrender to each other has brought them a rich, joy-filled rapport. Both have transcended the Aquarian inherent fear of intimacy and have realized that only when they descend from their ivory towers is it possible to emotionally unite with another.

One Aquarian challenge is to learn how to accept and live in an imperfect world. Their revolutionary sensibilities need to be channeled into championing healthy reform. Repugnance of conformity must be balanced with tolerance and understanding.

Their purpose is to manifest their ideals in the real world, but they can only do what they can do. Not yet perfected, what Aquarian lessons remain? Their ultra-cerebral, highly idealized minds have to learn to coexist with consensus reality and human imperfection. Just what tonic does the Water Bearer carry? This liquid magic awakens us from our slumbers of complacent insularity. The infinite well of Aquarius gives of itself freely and unconditionally. The collective mind swells. Consider these Aquarians: author Eckhart Tolle and media mogul Oprah Winfrey—the perfect expressions of the Aquarian archetype.

Aries has given us a self; Taurus, our very essence; Gemini, our mind and ability to think and communicate. Cancer has endowed us with a wonderful, homey nest. Leo has given us the confidence to emote. Virgo, through its hard work, has brought us into a concise, working self to be proud of. Libra and Scorpio have given us companions and taught us true dedication. Sagittarius has greatly expanded our experience as our world grows exponentially. Capricorn has set the bar even higher as we take our place amongst our peers, and because of Aquarius we now act with group interests in mind and aspire to greater ideals that benefit all of mankind. This archetype naturally sees itself as an individual and part of the group at the same time. Your needs and mankind's needs are the same. Enlightened self-interest.

Aquarius truly represents the bridge between the world and beyond. The existential conundrum of this sign is that individuation has been the goal all along and is still necessary, yet this very independent and distinct self reveals itself as the illusion that now has to be transcended.

Back in the Newtonian world of "this versus that," Aquarius simply could not relate. Because of this, most people can't understand their higher vision.

Capricorn is Newtonian-linear.
Aquarius is multidimensional-quantum-Self.
Pisces is Oneness-undifferentiated-non-Self.

We are nearing our final stage—the only one left—the original and final frontier. Like a Möbius strip, in the stage of Aquarius we see that oneness and individuality *appear* as two diametrically opposite forces that are alchemically melded together. In the final stage of Pisces, individuality is seen for the silly dream that it is and has been all along. We are now compelled to take a leap of faith without the burden of self.

The ultimate paradox is that there never really was one.

"For whoever wants to save his life will lose it,
but whoever loses his life (for me) will save it."

—Luke 9:23-24

Pisces: Isn't That Silly?

At last we arrive at Pisces, the ultimate sign of the zodiac—not that it's the best or superior to other signs but it *is* the ultimate. Pisces can no longer afford the weight of the self. In Pisces we transcend self-hood and reach for the truly spiritual and unfathomable. At the archetypal level, *all the other signs are contained within Pisces.* By all means, this does not imply that every Pisces that you know has it together.

What, to our amazement, do we see when we analyze the last sign? It's "mutable and water." Our final sign must be expressed in a mutable, giving way and the element of water (or, love) is the most fluid. The inherent intelligence of the zodiac has been evolving towards this step since stage one. Pisces continues to spread the life-giving waters of Aquarius to all. Love is the magic solution. Pisces' very heart is the essential need to give unconditional love to all. It's the apex of all archetypes, the Hero's destination. The Hero disappears into his sojourn and his evolutionary culmination brings closure to this age-old circle—another reason why the zodiac is exquisite.

No sign has the urge to be as open and accepting as the Fish. Aries follows the self's instincts; Taurus, their desires. Gemini is intrigued by ever new mental titillations; Cancer, their emotional needs. Leo instinctively needs to express itself while Virgos keep busy perfecting their skills. Libras and Scorpios are usually quite tied up with their partners. Sagittarians are generally too busy exploring and having fun to worry about anything, while Capricorn is doing the opposite. As for Aquarius, they are usually quite occupied assembling the entire mental anagram of life.

In this final quadrant and last sign of the "other-oriented" signs, Pisces is ready to transcend all things. Their goal is non-duality, oneness.

> *As Zen Buddhism insists, all things must be given up.*

Aquarius eventually discovers that the Big Universal Puzzle cannot be solved through objective thought, for it would always be stuck in a dual, polar universe. By default, there can be no separateness in a world that is one. Now, the self must be surrendered completely in order to continue along the arduous path to enlightenment. *This is why it's so hard for devotees to succeed in a Piscean incarnation.* Unity can only come from unconditional acceptance, non-discrimination, inclusion and non-resistance; this is the Piscean domain. Now we can easily see how the Aquarian conquest of paradoxes paved the way for this final metamorphosis.

In many cases when I have a Piscean person in my office, I spend the first half hour explaining to them *what* they are (astrologically speaking, of course). They are "raised" among eleven other signs of the zodiac that defend their own storylines.

> *To most signs, personal storyline is everything;*
> *to Pisces, personal storyline is a silly fable;*
> *they're just not that concerned about it.*

Pisces' ruler is Neptune, the planet in astrology whose essence is so hard to capture. It does not support worldly activity or individual progress.

> *As always we tire*
> *Of the silence of Neptune*
> *Never loud or even proud*
> *No promises made soon*
>
> *Its mystery is simple*
> *No koan can contain*
> *Its form or its wishes*
> *For as it loses, it gains*

The inherent wisdom of Pisces is that in giving we truly receive. Most enlightened personages echo this same sentiment. They see *beyond individuality.* "Judge not and ye shall not be judged." This is not a mandate for good behavior; it is a major perspective of a truly spiritual life. When one judges, one sees separateness, therefore missing the unity of life. Unless more critical placements of planets are found in their natal chart, most born to Pisces hardly ever judge others. It's simply not the nature of the Fish.

Every holy book I have ever read says that separateness is an illusion. This is not just a pretty, flowery chorus but a declaration of the true nature of reality. Therefore, in a world that is based in separateness (92 percent non-Piscean,) Pisceans often have difficulty because they have nothing to be competitive about. They instinctively get that all people are truly equal. They are born with deep-rooted faith and belief in the Divine even if they have a hard time articulating it. When we follow the lead of this wisest of signs, we begin to truly see. Spiritual teacher Ram Dass once said:

> *"If you really want to be someone, then be nobody special and you can be whomever you want."*

When you reach inside of a Pisces, you'll find that there's nothing there to be found; that's because they're *everywhere*, unbounded. You can't restrict Pisces because they're not constructed the same as the other eleven. It's actually funny to think that a football team has eleven members. Symbolically, Pisces sits on the sidelines. How apropos. That's their place: one foot in this world, one foot out; two fish swimming in opposite directions. They follow *spirit*—it's that simple. They *are* spirit, or soul. Therefore, Pisces cannot truly be assigned to any cosmic stage of man. They are beyond man; their essence is man/god, if you will.

So, what do I mean by the "ultimate sign?" Simply put, things go effortlessly around Pisceans because they don't default to whiny self-needs. They don't think of themselves; they think of others. One of the best examples I've ever used is the one of the mama cat caught in a fire. She goes back into the flames to save her young, only to perish herself. *This is Pisces.* This is their nature, the way they function at a deep archetypal level. It is oftentimes sad to see how they can be treated by the other signs. Others mislabel their gentle passivity as weakness. Some people see them as having no backbone when, in fact, they simply don't want more than their share—if even that much.

The Pisces archetype is a state of consciousness: "The meek shall inherit the earth" refers to those who aren't hung up on ego-advancement. Pisces can't help feeling non-ambitious unless other forces in the chart lie contrary. They don't want to "get ahead" in life; doing so is futile to them. To a Pisces, futility equals more money, more sex, bigger house, better job, nicer car. None of these things are going to bring them to Heaven, and Jesus clearly told us that Heaven *is a state of being* within each of us. It's not a place you visit or a material object that you acquire; it's something you already have.

How can you advance past the fact that you're already all things?

In many ways, Pisces is the most challenging sign of the zodiac to be, and most never come close to actualizing this pinnacle of potentialities. In my mind, Jesus was the most vivid representation of this state of elevated consciousness. He knew who He was; He had Himself *in perspective.* "Thy will, not my will." He understood. "I and my Father are One." *There can be no unity until there is surrender of self.* Then, all is gained.

> *He kept saying it: "of Myself, I (self) can do nothing, it all comes from my Father (non-self)" . . . or the Absolute, the Unmanifest, the Zero-Field, the Nagual, the Field of Intention, whatever you want to call It.*

Similar to the preceding paradigm of Aquarius, Pisces is also full of paradoxes, which is another indication of advanced attainment. Yielding versus succumbing. Surrendering versus being dominated. Being compassionate versus being a martyr. All of these are issues that the Fish must resolve. Serving others from a position of strength and choice is completely different than doing so out of low self-esteem.

Pisces experiences the freedom of unboundedness between people but at the same time can suffer the invasion of their own sovereignty (ego). By definition, one cannot be dual and non-dual at the same time. Therein lies the *cross that is borne* of all developing selves at their respective Piscean passage.

> *The trick is to be a self and a non-self simultaneously.*

Many times Pisceans have poor judgment when it comes to relationships; after all, theirs is the impulse of non-discrimination. When it comes to Pisces and their choice of partners, it is extremely common for their friends to say, "Where did you find *that* person?" It's simply that they don't see differences; they see what's the same. God love 'em! Pisces see no disparities because there really aren't any.

Pisces drifts and floats with the currents. "Wherever life takes me, that's fine." This attitude can be good or bad (if such a polarity actually exists). Listlessness is common among Pisces, along with escapism, alcoholism and drug abuse. They have a powerful need to elude anything that is earthbound, such as personal problems, job responsibilities, confrontations, competition, and any and all types of struggle. Instead of landing them in fountains of euphoria, this often lands them in lots of hot water.

Speaking of hot water, I tried to "date" a Pisces girl during my college days. She came to my apartment one day to fix me spaghetti. As the water was boiling, she stepped outside for a minute. I saw her a month later. Some subtle zephyr had simply whisked her away.

Now how, I ask you, can we expect this final sign to even consider personal consequences? This amorphous, indefinable and nebulous Magic Bus that we call Pisces is akin to the spaceship that has left earth. Free of Gaia's pull, it floats away and disappears beyond our grasp, laws and bounds.

Pisces transcends the zodiac's gravity.

Fish have a very big problem with a very small word: "No." They just can't say no. This is *the* sign that is prone to guilt. "Surely there must be something I could have done"; that's how they see it. I call it the hanging-on-the-cross syndrome. "I can hang on the cross for another day or month . . . for you." Many times they experience guilt for even existing! You can see where this comes from. Commonly, if they do anything for themselves they feel badly. That means they have gone too far with selflessness. People sense it, too, and the loving nature of Pisces gets taken advantage of constantly. Another key to living a healthy Piscean existence is not getting confused between doing the will of *other people* and doing "His" will. When they fall prey to the former, they often become enslaved.

Unfortunately, this can lead them into playing the role of the *victim*. What's that common saying? "There are no victims, only volunteers." When this vulnerable sign is surrounded by those who are more than well armed, sometimes it seems as if their only recourse is to yield. After all, these pacifists feel that they can't fight back or promote themselves. To this sign, assertiveness feels like aggressiveness. Ironically, the solution for Pisces is that they must learn to develop a strong ego.

Pisces favorite saying is, "It doesn't matter." It can be quite telling when Pisces uses the word "silly" to describe other's errant behavior. They naturally have great compassion for all as we get temporarily lost along the way. Our foibles are not to be condemned. Pisces would say: "Oops, aren't they silly?"

This final stage of Pisces is demanding, requiring total surrender. While the small "you" is being transcended, the larger "You" is becoming full of being. It's such a difficult level from which to graduate because you can't take anything with you. Total dedication and allegiance to Oneness is required. There are bigger fish to fry.

The final stage of the zodiac is beyond thought. It is to be *experienced*; you can *be* It, but not by *thinking about It*. This ineffable state of consciousness transcends the finest efforts of Aquarius. Aquarian intellectual constructs can only grow larger and more complex. They must necessarily yield to the simplified field of Pisces in which nothing matters anymore, because everything matters equally.

> *It's only maddening if you think about it, and*
> *thinking has little place in this dimension.*

The inherent wisdom of The Beatle's song "Let It Be" tells the whole story. When we accept the nature of all things, we resist nothing and are left with the emptiness of fullness.

I truly believe that each sign of the zodiac has one simple need. In the case of Pisces, their need is simply *to be left alone*. They just want to float in the sea of undifferentiated Allness. They want to call it a wrap with this world of limits and bodies and tight blue jeans. Their aim is not to be aimless; they specifically and solely want to follow the Holy Spirit's compass of true north.

This archetype is the final stage of the zodiac: sublimity.

At the end of this colorful spectrum, the zodiacal wheel culminates. Where does the evolving self go from here? Nowhere! It came from nowhere and everywhere. It never "left" in the first place. There never was anywhere to go. It was all an Arian dream! As a hypnotherapist friend says, "What if I existed separately from everything else?" Without time or space, *Pisces simply gives up the illusion by which it was hypnotized during the first eleven phases.* This final, elusive Zen state of no-thingness is difficult to attain.

> *"abandon abandon*
> *even your dear self*
> *abandon"*
>
> *—Rumi*

Now the canvas is empty, free of the excess baggage of the self. In the quiet stillness of nothingness, in the black emptiness of non-personhood, a new embryonic field lies latent. It's time for another dream, a field of possibilities and promise, a new churning, yearning sea of potential manifestation longing to be, to unfold once again, to love anew.

Let there be light! And thusly Aries the Ram ignites once again and grants us its life spark—as Carlos Castaneda called it, "*A tremor in the air.*" It's the initial ember of life, and we are all born again, only to go round and round on this sacred wheel of life, this Exquisite Zodiac.

Polishing The Diamond: A Sign-by-Sign Delineation of the Zodiac's Six Archetypal Variants

You've probably gotten a sense by now that the twelve signs of the zodiac differ in many ways. We've taken a look at the primary archetypes of each sign. Now let's slice the pie into smaller pieces by getting into more depth about the six archetypal variants that we briefly previewed in Part I. These variants explain most of what makes a sign like it is, as well as what differentiates one from another.

For your ease of reading, here are the six archetypal variants again:

> The Twelve Stages of Man
>
> Each Sign as an Outgrowth of Previous Stage
>
> The Three Modes and Four Elements
>
> Self-Oriented versus Other-Oriented Signs
>
> The Six Polarities
>
> The Ruling Planets

The Twelve Stages of Man

The early signs of the zodiac represent the innocent, inexperienced and purest form of a being that will eventually grow more complex throughout the remainder of the twelve signs.

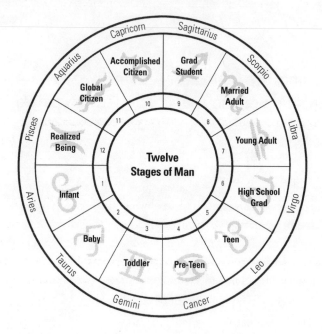

The stages of man that we are discussing here are conceptual, archetypal and symbolic. The wheel of life simply cannot exist and sustain itself without a healthy blend of these *younger* and *older* energy blueprints. It is similar to what we see in nature: a plant is born, grows, produces, fades and finally dies, giving way to the new again. Life's cycles are ever present throughout the backbone of most astrological principles.

In the same fashion as we observe the young of our race, we give them special consideration in exchange for their purity, innocence and refreshing view of the world. Likewise, we appreciate the elders of the zodiac for their patience, experience and wisdom. We need both not only collectively but within our own personal development.

When you start to see basic astrology operating just in this one archetypal variant of the Twelve Stages of Man, you'll be amazed at how much your relationships begin to make sense almost immediately. Below, as you go through each sign, keep in mind that we are addressing the pure center in each sign that gives each one its archetypal core.

Aries is clearly the stage of the **infant**. Its demands are paramount and need to be met "right now!" In general, the Aries archetype is basically only aware of itself. Of course Aries people are aware of others yet they have to satisfy their own needs first. Self-focus is not the same as being selfish; there is quite a difference. Being selfish is when you are aware of others but still want more than your share. Aries are mainly self-focused.

Aries is simply innocent. This explains why they are so enamored with themselves, and it also explains why they simply can't deal with delays or obstacles. It's not the infant's fault that they have immediate needs; it's just the way it is. This young essence makes Aries fond of babies and contributes to their youthful appearance well into their senior years.

Aries is refreshing, just like a baby, because of their freshness, newness, innocence and guileless behavior. What you see is what you get with this paradigm. They launch the zodiac and are symbolically at a stage of seeking direct life experience. They want to see what they can do.

Taurus is symbolic of the **baby,** just a bit past the newborn. It represents the stage where the baby has learned to be comfortable by itself and has become much more patient. Its world is still relatively small at this stage as the young one enjoys holding its blanket, its toys, its body, anything it can grab onto.

This stage learns that there is more beyond its own existence. Because of this primal development, Taurus has always been associated with money, collections, value and self-worth. It just makes sense that the "self" grabs and holds onto its "things" at this stage. Many times the word "stubborn" is paired to the sign of Taurus. Have you ever tried to take a toy from a baby? (That settles that matter!) Would you call the baby stubborn? No, the toy is an extension of their very being; therefore, losing a toy presents Taurus with a feeling of loss or death and is to be avoided.

Taurus is comfortable living with relatively little. They don't need their world to be large and are, in fact, uncomfortable beyond their known surroundings. Don't be fooled, much is happening at this stage as the entity is preparing to encounter exponential growth and acclimation. The relationship of "self" to "thing" is being studied. Outside influences are considered distractions because the baby gets overwhelmed with too many options.

They want their defined physical space, too, and they don't want it to be changed! Their place gives them a sense of reference and physical stability—a very important need of the Bull.

Gemini. A huge evolutionary leap is made at this stage of the **toddler** as the entity has learned that it can cruise, explore, communicate and ask questions. No wonder Geminis are known for their inability to sit still. Their incessant impulse is to look over here, look over there; the world is made up of zillions of interesting items and ideas. In a very basic way, Gemini begins the observation of its own mind, as they are fascinated with everything.

Because the whirlwinds of curiosity are blowing so strongly at this stage, one cannot expect this young child to corral the ideas into a larger conceptual framework. This is why they can seem scattered or shallow. Geminis are happy to hop from one mental sandbox to another. "Say, what do you have in yours?"

In one way, this is a very difficult archetype to be. Gemini can't help its youthful nature and should be quite proud of it; however, just like a child who wants to be seen as being more grown up, they're simply not ready. This doesn't necessarily apply to the Gemini Sun signs you might know; such might not be the case when you get a complete reading on the birth chart with all the other planets and signs considered.

The Twins are matched to the proverbial butterfly, bouncing from one flower to another, getting fascinated then onto the rest of the dale. They need to be left alone. They have to live in this mythical "grown-up" world and study it. "Why is everyone taking things so seriously?" The great accomplishments of this stage are that evolving man grows greatly both mentally and in its ability to talk and interact.

Cancer is a touchy stage, indicative of the **pre-teen**. Delicate and tender, this fourth sign is caught between being comfortable in the burrow and knowing it must leave some day. That's what Cancer is all about: the tug between dependency and independence.

This age intuits that the world is a good place but is also keenly aware of its dangers. It is a scary temporary passage where the child is really confused about where to hang on, but the child isn't at all sure *if* they can make it on their own. Above all, emotional development must be encouraged.

In many ways, Cancer is an "in between" stage beyond babyhood yet not ready to go it alone. They no longer need to frantically explore but are not yet ready to fledge the nest; they are in need of the family but not prepared to open the door to others. It's a tough stage, a cardinal stage, and quite necessary. The "evolving self" is growing up.

Leo is the **teenager**. As with any teenager, they demand that you show them respect that may or may not have been earned. The Lion picks up from where Cancer left off and dares to leave the comfort of home with great pride and courage. Leo's job now is to reach beyond and grow in confidence. This uncomfortable stage of the teen is fraught with uncertainty, as it competes with its peers in order to make itself feel okay.

Leo has a delicate balance to achieve: 1) it can't return to the hypersensitivity of Cancer, 2) it has to hold its own at its new stage even though it hasn't quite yet developed enough self-assuredness, and 3) it must operate with confidence without getting lost in an inflated self-view. Many Leos get lost in the trap of feeling superior.

Leo really represents the final "childhood" stage, where much is learned and accomplished. Now, it must turn the evolving being over to the archetype of Virgo's finishing school.

Virgo. One might think of this parallel to mankind as the **high school graduate**. This chapter is about putting it all together and taking ownership of what the entity is and is not. Self-honesty is paramount at this juncture.

Virgo has transcended all of the earlier developmental stages and prepares itself for adulthood. Maturity is the major word here, as it has to stop making excuses for any of its slip-ups and prepare to be responsible for its behavior.

Growing up is a bitch.

This stage is not yet quite ready for partnership but is doing everything it can to prepare for it. Being Virgo is much like attending the prom. You're looking good, which is the result of years of hard work; now you just need to dance on your own two feet.

Virgo lets go of much of the drama of self-absorption in order to concentrate on making itself ready to meet others as a young adult. Virgo does not want to embarrass itself as it enters the next stage of the socialite.

Libra is symbolic of the **young adult** in every sense of the word. The self has made it into the world and now sets its goal on being accepted by society. The entire focus now becomes, "How do I behave in this world? Who am I compared to others?" Thanks to the hard, unselfish work accomplished during the Virgo phase, Libra is now free to represent the cardinal quality once again as it leads Cosmic Man to take its place alongside its partner in the community.

We have now crossed into the "we" half of the zodiac and the developing entity needs the sounding-board potential of a partner. The young adult is quite inexperienced in this larger domain but is equipped and eager to explore fresh possibilities. Libra eagerly engages in relationships as it reflects off of the "other," making great use of its charms, poise and tact.

Scorpio matches the title of **married adult** better than Libra. The Libra stage is one of partnership; Scorpio is the stage where the self is more prepared for true marriage. Picking up where Libra left off, the cosmic entity is now ready for the deep commitment that nuptials require. Intimacy and truly belonging to one another is Scorpio's *raison d'être*. Can we actually belong to another or is this a figment of a romantic dream?

Either way, the path of the Scorpion is an intense one where relationships are taken very seriously. The adult is growing up quickly but is still somewhat limited in the vision and breadth of experience that awaits.

Sagittarius is the **grad student** traveling abroad. It transcends Scorpio's steamy soap opera and off to university it goes, out to see the world and meet others from around the globe. Travel is huge to this archetype as it represents the broadening of the grander self's experience.

The Archer aims high and is very idealistic. Sag has a burning need to expand in all directions, and education is one of its primary needs. Thus, the adult now is married, educated and ready to graduate from college and take its place in the world.

Capricorn is the **accomplished citizen**. Our final cardinal sign assumes leadership as the wise elder. Steeped in a strong sense of obligation, Caps give back to the world by assuring that our social and cultural wheels keep functioning smoothly. This sign is known as the "old man" in the zodiac, mainly because it is ruled by "Old Man Saturn." The Goat is the fatherly shepherd of the zodiac.

This is the stage where we are expected to have gained common sense. This stage can be likened to that of a human's experience around age 58 when they are experiencing their second Saturn return. At this stage, man has paid his dues to his family and culture and is preparing to retire and offer his wisdom to ensuing generations.

Aquarius, the **philanthropist** or **global citizen** represents a higher octave of Capricorn. The entity is not so concerned with maintaining its position or status. Now, the Water Bearer gives back to its world, strongly appreciative of the very Earth, and becomes a committed campaigner for its conservation.

Aquarius has the keenest vision of the dozen as it looks to the future. Protective of its individual rights yet just as passionate in what we can accomplish as an ensemble, Aquarius is the epitome of possibility and idealism, what mankind can do when it unites in common cause.

Pisces is the **spiritual leader** or **realized being**. Although many Pisces can seem quite childlike, they're actually more representative of being ageless, beyond time and form. Enigmatically, this final sign contains all twelve archetypes within. Its youthful sense emanates from its pure innocence and lack of resistance. Pisces-the-spiritual-master is full of wisdom and quiet faith, not dogma, bravado or piety.

Pisces is beyond the beyonds, mysterious and timeless, formless as spirit, unpredictable as a quantum particle, and pinpointed only by its amorphous nature: empty, void and full.

And so it goes in the astrological cycle of life—the wheel goes round and round, and the young follow the old in this, the Exquisite Zodiac.

Each Sign as an Outgrowth of Previous Stage

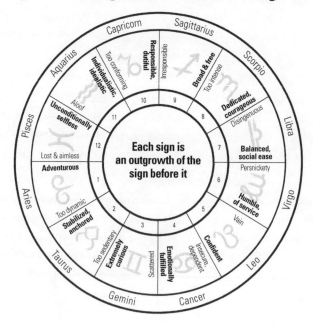

As stated earlier, each sign is an outgrowth of the sign that precedes it. This criterion is perhaps the most important of the previously discussed archetypal variants. In many ways, this really explains *why* each sign has its compelling urge to do what it does. This is why the Pisces wants to abandon Aquarius' newly found "individuality." It is why Virgo wants to be "second fiddle" compared to Leo's need for the limelight, and so on.

Each sign has a job to do and fully expresses the archetype upon which it is based. Each blossoms in its own regard as it develops its critical chapter of the zodiac. There comes a time, however, when a sign's overall function ceases to evolve and something new must morph out of its status quo. It's almost as if the sign says, "Been there, done that." As each sign of the zodiac conquers its charge and masters its state, a natural transformation stands before it.

All signs seem to have a natural intolerance for the energy that came before it. They need to transcend, go beyond and represent almost the exact opposite of what was accomplished previously. Thus, we are blessed with healthy diversity among the heavenly dozen. All archetypes build upon their previous successes and transform into the next with a new element, a new mode, and other characteristics.

Aries. This principle "outgrowth" is difficult to see in this sign. Why? Although it *appears* to be the first sign, in actuality it is the beginning of another lap around the cosmic circle—another revolution, all emanating from the emptiness and fullness of the previous ocean of Pisces.

Remember, Pisces focused on the non-self as it returned to the Allness. Along comes Aries with an excited outburst. Life evolves out of the "nothingness" or, as the Bible says, "out of the void." Let there be light! . . . and there was. Life has a burning need *to exist*, to matter and to experience itself. So, it invents its own delusion of separateness (Aries) and we start down the road to the next eleven dream states (the other signs) until we "remember" and return to Oneness once again. Around and around we go.

Aries explodes onto the scene with a great sense of "self" yet is based in the unconscious state of losing its vision *of the whole* and becomes solely focused upon the small "I".

The ego is born— the imaginary sense of independent, separated self.

Becoming… remembering… surrendering…

In this innocent primordial Aries state, the self is all concerned with how it is doing, how it gets what it wants, only able to see life through its own perspective. What else can it do? It has "had enough" of this being nothing, this sense of non-individuation, and longs for experience in order to validate itself. Through Aries, the Cosmic Man is born again with an undeterred excitement for life, with great enthusiasm for the limitless possibilities that lie ahead.

We now understand why Aries is bold, courageous and known for being a pioneer. We see why they know what they want and seek adventure in all that they do. The Ram needs its buttressed horns on its brow in order to charge ahead into the great unknown!

After some time, Aries masters this primal state. This premier archetype has burgeoned into a shiny new being. What else can be done now? Aries can't just continue to charge about. The Ram can no longer conquer and subsist on adventures alone. It must be slowed, anchored into a firmer sense of self—one with substance—then it must get some rest and plant itself amongst its surroundings. The developing archetype must be moored to something less incendiary, less meteoric, and find a constant place in which to *be*, such as the earth itself . . . and thus, the sign of Taurus is born.

Taurus lends a firm hand. It can't keep burning up in space like a comet. Now the need has turned into a mandatory urge to affix itself by sending out roots. "Stop all this crazy jumping around and settle down!" says Taurus. And Taurus is serious, too.

One can feel the sigh of relief, "Ahhhhhh," as Taurus slows down and starts to make sense out of its new role and surroundings. Patience is now the new firmament. This sign grows slowly and steadily. Its roots burrow deep because its plans are permanent. The Bull is as patient as Aries is impatient, like the tortoise and the hare. It learns to wait and has respect for the slow, steady growth taking place in its relatively small, pleasing garden.

Famous for its sense of smell, touch and taste, Taurus takes time to not only smell the roses but savor the essence of all things. So much was missed by the previous sign. Don't rush Taurus! They are busy learning and staking out their territory in the newfound Eden. People born with much of this quintessential energy feel charred and scorched by exuberant, extroverted fire people. To Taurus, it's senseless to keep flying off the handle when one could enjoy being home and relishing the cornucopia of the yield.

During this second stage of the zodiac, we begin to ascertain the *value* found in all things. Taurus has not only grounded its world but has organized and claimed it for itself.

Now Cosmic Man learns of a sense called "mine."

Therefore, Taurus is to be ever known as possessive and fixed. Granted, it has gained much during its passage through this secondary phase; however, left to itself, its inert life threatens stagnancy and decay. The time has come to morph once again. The self has become too cramped and immobile. It just can't go on like this. Look out, here comes Gemini!

Gemini. Bored to tears, Gemini not only splinters in two but has developed a complete sense of repugnancy towards anything static. Taurus hates change; Gemini thrives on it. With a new zest, they yearn for fresh air, exploration and diversification, eager to sample life's smorgasbord.

Curiosity is the word.

The self has been compressed into a stuffy cabin fever that propels the Twins into a spiral of tremendous activity. They cannot imagine staying put in the same ole chair, watching the same ole TV reruns and eating the same ole food. Variety is the spice of life for Geminis.

Through Gemini, the self expands greatly out into the world of minutiae, the field of new ideas. We must remember and appreciate that it can afford to do so because it now has a platform from which to launch—namely, the rock-solid base of Taurus.

As with all of the signs, we benefit from the previous sign and are simultaneously filled with a compulsion to transcend the same. Because of Taurus, Gemini can land and rest but it doesn't want to, and it can't rest for long—that's how enthusiastic their desire for information gathering has become. To the Twins, no subject is off limits. What can appear to be a generic scanning of the world's database really does justify us calling Gemini the zodiac's "info depot." That's what they are, and that's what they do. The universal mind is awakening!

Needless to say, there finally comes a time when bouncing from one data portal to another has to cease. Is it simply because the growing entity needs something else at this time? We notice now after these first three signs that there has been, as of yet, no baptism in water. Aries is enchanted with itself for its simple existence. Taurus is quite busy in its orchards, thank you. And Gemini has thousands of partially read books piled up on its end tables.

Along comes Cancer—a major step—the first sign to experience emotion, and the first to feel vulnerable and imbed itself within family representing the final element of water.

Cancer. The developing self is hungry. It *needs*, and I'm not talking about food. I'm talking about emotional sustenance. What Gemini found "interesting" no longer interests Cancer. What good is fascination with trivia going to do when the Cancerian is naked, exposed and needs emotional support? Cancer can no longer rely upon its mind now as it did in the third stage. Now, it's all about the heart: being wanted, safe, nurtured and loved.

Thus the impetus for the family unit comes about. Cancer soothes and tames the ever restless mind. As it nurtures its nestlings, it nurtures itself. We now have representatives from each of the four elements: fire, earth, air and finally, water. With this influx of water, the grander entity starts to experience quite a *growth spurt*. The natural inclination now is to get far away from the logic of the left brain. Cancer has seen the world thanks to the innocent explorations of the Twins. Inadvertently, it now has an all-too-real appreciation of how dangerous the world can be. This is why many Cancerians seem hard and aloof when in actuality, they're just protecting their soft underbelly by being somewhat defensive.

Just think about it: all of this rudimentary "stuff"
from Aries and Taurus and Gemini gets dumped on Cancer
like we dump our laundry onto our mothers' laps.

Cancer now *knows* that it is vulnerable. When one is at risk, one becomes cautious. It needs buffering; it needs family. The Crab is developing a very important element that has to carry Cosmic Woman all the way to the end of the zodiacal spectrum. The *mothering instinct* surfaces in this archetypal pattern as the inherent need to protect becomes foremost.

The developing self has now come a long way in this mythical chapter. It has a new self in Aries; it gains senses and extensions of self in Taurus, its mind in Gemini, and is now comfortably protected and fostered in the sign of the Mother. Ideas of the mind have become a distant memory at this stage.

The evolving entity is becoming more complete. Even so, it is not by any means comfortable baring itself to a world full of hazards. And what exactly are those hazards? Others who are not sensitive to their state of being. Evolution must continue; the Crab can't stay shrink-wrapped forever and it knows that it must gain the courage to come out and test the waters. It has to establish the confidence to survive in this dog-eat-dog world. The time has come to boldly expose itself and take ownership of its domain; thus, the jungle and the Lion.

Leo. Shaken and excited by its exodus, Leo holds its head high and lets out a roar of dominance over its new sphere of influence. It has grown discomfited by the timidity of Cancer and requires itself now to reach deep and find its own strength. Pride becomes the driving force as Leo looks to show that it can handle its new domain. It tests itself continuously here in this fifth stage. Still reeling from its recent departure from the den, Leo disavows this fact and demands that no one sees it—but the emperor has no clothes. This is why Leo can easily get into denial and absolutely demands respect for its hard-won dignity.

Respect is absolutely the fuel that drives Leo.

This explains every single thing about Leo. It doesn't matter what Leo does, it's how they do it. They must be seen now as capable of standing on their own. Leo is a larger-than-life character and no longer wants anything to do with hypersensitivity and bashfulness. And roar it does!

Leo can take one of two forks in the road. The noble road is where it shines as it graciously accepts kudos with head held high, not letting pride overshadow self-realism. Down the other fork lies difficulty because the Leo's pride and exaggerated sense of entitlement can become the be-all and end-all.

During this valiant stage, the evolving entity greatly expands its being. Now it proudly displays all of its brilliant peacock feathers. Confidence expands greatly and the growing self is more capable than ever of mixing it up in its new milieu. Even so, however faint, inside every Leo is a lingering Cancer. This will explain much about Leo to you. They're not as tough as they want you to think.

In one way or another, every sign wants to disidentify with the sign before it.

Growth must continue. Each sign tires of its story, no matter how glorious. Each archetype can only carry on to a point where change again becomes mandatory. For Leo, bravado, haughtiness and even a healthy amount of swagger no longer satisfies. Real humility is now necessary for evolution to continue through its future challenges. Leo has taken us far but it can go no further until it changes its tune. The first five signs have done much to develop Cosmic Man into a more complex being; now, refinement and integration are the necessary ingredients to add to this celestial broth during the distillation process called Virgo.

Virgo. Nothing could be truer in astrology than stating the degree to which Virgo abhors bluster. Behind the scenes is the place where they are comfortable. Yes, Leo has shown us great improvement in its ability to handle personal consequences; now Virgo, the expert, wants *no* notice or accolades. The Virgin feels humiliated in the spotlight. It has learned what false pride can do and no longer wants to toot that horn. Even so, because of the powerful surge of growth attributed to Leo,

Virgo can now perfect all the characteristics that it can before bridging to Libra and the second half of the zodiac. Virgo has to fix everything and make it shiny new.

Virgo wants the perfection of its work to stand on its own.

By exacting its always sharp mind, Virgo analytically spots all imperfections. Via Chiron, its ruler, they care to go the extra distance to purify all. Leo's job was to expand and grow confidence; now Virgo's is to clean up its act before the symbolic pairing with others. Benefiting from the new sense of certainty, Virgo takes on all comers. Gloating is not its thing; being of service is.

In general, no sign does its job better. Virgo's humility tends to hide the real value of their talents. Remember what I said earlier: if you're going to hire someone, hire a Virgo. Virgo is *the* sign that cares. This is the first sign of service to others and the Virgin was born to serve. It is the least self-oriented of the self-oriented signs. Virgo provides for others because it does what it must do.

It must get untangled from itself.
That is its only way out.

Remember that Chiron, Virgo's ruler, is a very unusual, mysterious minor planet/Centaur. It has only been known to us since 1977 and much is still to be discerned about this "bridge" to the outer planets. It resides between the inner planets—Sun through Saturn—and the outer impersonal planets of Uranus, Neptune and Pluto. Virgo/Chiron's need to bridge the gap between personal and non-personal planets typifies this "self" versus "other" orientation. It is the *bridge*. Virgo doesn't mind; its hope is to be an invisible and seamless link between the "me" and "we" halves of the circle.

The demarcation between the lower and upper halves of the zodiac starts to take place during the Virgo stage, not distinctly afterwards. By graduating from the self-involvement of the sign of Leo, Virgo takes us all much further by lessening its load of *self*—much like its polar opposite sign of Pisces.

So we can see why Virgo must do what it does. One can go on eternally finding *something* wrong in everything that it examines. The evolving status of Man can go no further by being the purifying perfectionist that it is. As with all the other eleven signposts, something must change with Virgo, as well. Eventually it must overcome its shyness and self-deprecation and make its debut among all the other stars in the sky in the sign of Libra.

Libra. While being tethered to the workbench in Virgo, Libra sensed that it missed out on much of the beauty and grace of life. Taking advantage of its new luster, Libra wants to intermingle with society. Virgo's hesitancy must now be transcended as this Cinderella stage of the self needs to see how it stacks up to its peers. The Scales symbolize *comparison*, and by contrasting oneself to others, one can get a sense of what one is; that's Libra. Virgo was satisfied blending into the background, clad in denim and a plaid shirt—not Libra. This sign is constantly focused on the latest styles and trends. How it looks to others in all ways is of main importance.

Libra now takes the opportunity to pair with another, something that archetypal Virgo was not prepared for. Just because Virgo serves others doesn't mean that it is able to fuse with another emotionally. Libra's nature isn't ready for that, really, but Libra is eager to find itself locked arm and arm during a pleasant night out. It's all about testing the waters for this sign. Recall how it was mentioned that Libra is the Aries of the second half of the zodiac? The development of partnership is of grand concern at this stage. Libra simply has to graduate from Virgoan micro-management in order to move into the world of companions with Venusian grace, tact and refinement.

Libra thoroughly enjoys its new position in life. Benefiting from all of the zodiac's previous accomplishments, this Venusian sign smoothly mingles with the "in crowd." Nothing is more important to Libra than being accepted socially.

Libra finds itself completely spellbound as it
moves in rhythm with the waltzing ballroom.

Libra has overcome Virgo's tendency towards coyness and reserve. Now, Cinderella realizes that, "No, it wasn't a dream after all. The glass slipper fits perfectly!"

Scorpio has had a good taste of partnership and now wants more. Based upon the social progress made in Libra, Scorpio is now ready to cast aside any and all personal reserve and go for it. It can no longer be satisfied with the trappings of a genteel relationship. This is precisely why this sign is so passionate. Lust, sex, devotion and stormy appetites take over. Scorpio can't stand anything that resembles weakness and to them, living with anything less than total devotion is just that.

Known for defying anyone or anything that might place social standards before their passions, they're going to be themselves, period. They know what they love and they know what they hate. No fence-sitting for this fixed water sign. At this rather late eighth stage, the archetype is no longer focused upon self-development and instead turns to transcending the self. The imperative now is to add one plus one and get something much greater than two. Evolution is really fired up.

There are many types of Scorpios but they all share one thing: intensity. Being an emotional sign, they turn a cold shoulder to their predecessor, Libra, because Scorpio is ready to risk it all. This most courageous of signs has high expectations of their mates, too. The Libra constitution was simply not ready for this much heat in the kitchen.

By the time the growing self has reached this stage, life is becoming very complicated with all the emotional freight. Many of us crave "soul satisfaction" or our "soul mate"—a perilous pursuit, for sure. If our partner changes—oops!—what happens to us? That's the very fear of both Libra and Scorpio.

So we see that the Scorpio experience can be one histrionic stage filled with great highs and lows. The evolving being certainly learns much here, but enough is enough. Few entities can withstand the unrelenting pressure and demands of this emotional alchemy. It has to come to an end before it self-combusts.

We have learned. The pain and sacrifices suffered in the two relationship archetypes are now behind us. No wonder Sagittarius wants to sit back, have fun and lighten its load.

Sagittarius. This transition is probably the easiest of all twelve to understand. Sag has just escaped from a burning building's inferno. Does it have to be so arduous? Certainly this ninth sign benefits greatly from the conquests of the previous two signs but it has had its fill of this *Wuthering Heights* in every relationship it encounters.

> *Passions, schmassions, Sag just wants to enjoy life!*
> *After all, why are we here?*

This advancing entity wants to break out, expand, explore and not be encumbered by restrictions. The self-flagellation of Scorpio has tempered Cosmic Man into a courageous lot ready to climb to the top of the zodiac; now it can take on all comers. Sagittarius knows Capricorn is next as the Archer aims his arrow towards the summit. Sagittarius is the one sign that you can always count "in" no matter what you are doing. Their effervescent, cheerful sense of optimism is more than catchy. Fired by the aftermath of Scorpio's pent-up passions, Sag lets loose.

Yes, Sagittarius is known for its clumsy and carefree nature. They have thrown caution to the wind; no more self-restriction. Being happy-go-lucky is not intended to imply irresponsibility and coldness, although it sometimes does manifest that way. Mostly, it means that their built-in zeal is based upon being unfettered and free.

Remember, Sagittarius is ruled by free-spirited Jupiter. Meanwhile, next door, Scorpio is dominated by Pluto and Capricorn is regulated by stern Saturn. That says it all. It's absolutely no wonder that Sag is like it is. They know of restrictions; they've heard about them *somewhere* but limiting themselves is far from their nature. Yes, the sign of the half-man/half-horse is wild. Honesty is their flying carpet. Scorpio was so measured and upcoming Capricorn is so cautious in speech. Not Sagittarius; open mouth, insert foot.

> *But every party must end.*

Capricorn. Now, this sign really has issues with the sign before it! Sag knew the fun would end someday but who wanted to face it? We couldn't keep borrowing and borrowing. Eventually we had to come down off of our high horse. Hello, Capricorn! Yes, poor old, abused, unappreciated Capricorn. Just think of it: Now we are expected to pay our bills and become responsible for our behavior? How absolutely dismal and unjust!

As mentioned earlier, Capricornian discipline and self-regulation couldn't be further from the nature of the buoyant and breezy Centaur. Capricorn not only prides itself in its self-sacrificing sense of conformity, it understands that sobering, mature tendencies must come about in order for us to truly shepherd our world.

This is why Capricorn is known as the father of the zodiac.

Someone has to do it.

Imbued with this reserved nature, Capricorn is actually thinking on a much bigger scale than before. The sign of the Goat considers the proper functioning of the whole society. Granted, Capricorn sacrifices the self-interest of fiery Sagittarius. If not for the Goat, the decay of neglect would contaminate the social structure that is Capricorn's domain. One thing you can be sure of, the sign whose motto is "make sure" is not going to let decay occur on its watch. Call it painful, call it limitation, call it whatever you want to; Capricorn will face up to its responsibilities. Some avoid visiting the dentist, whereas Capricorn will submit to the root canal.

Needless to say, this self-restriction and obedience to laws can only go so far. Life's inner fire wants out again and can't escape when it is always confined by propriety.

Sagittarius is the spirit of the law; Capricorn, the letter of the law.

The heavy degree of conformity that was necessary in order to transcend Sagittarius is the very same constraint that adds to Capricorn's sense of imprisonment. The soul eventually has to be freed; thus, we morph once again—this time, into Aquarius.

Aquarius. One job for the Aquarian is to recover the free self that was forfeited as it was leaving Sagittarius. Yes, Capricorn has "done everything right" but that's the problem! Aquarius is here to break the mold. We all benefited from the maturation of the Goat, but Aquarius is to maximize its individuality. Now, it follows only the beat of its own drummer.

Yes, Capricorn was the first archetypal period where the evolving entity put global needs ahead of itself. Now, the Water Bearer wants to give back by showering its life-giving waters across the globe. No sign is more humanitarian or quite as idealistic. This eleventh stop along the zodiacal highway changes its focus to the health of the collective. Preparing for the ultimate and final stage of Pisces, this sign dreams of what we can all do if we work in unison.

Unlike Capricorn, which follows standard procedure, Aquarius thinks way outside of the box. Capricorn had to align itself with social structure in order to make the society a working whole but the box was an illusion after all. Now, Aquarius goes one step better. It paves the way into the future as its powerful mindset figures out all the implications of implementing change.

What's going on in this stage is that Aquarius is starting to lift off the ground. All of the ten signs preceding it have had the charge of birthing, growing, establishing, developing, perfecting and partnering—all in an effort to climax at the top of the mountain. Cosmic Man gained the zenith, seated in the throne of worldly success, if you will. Aquarius goes one step farther: It knows that man cannot stand alone so it outstretches its arms and mind to include everyone equally (think of Abraham Lincoln). Man is eventually reaching back to God from whence he came. The Water Bearer gets just as high from other's accomplishments as it does from its own. By identifying with the group, the evolving self has now begun to transcend the individual and think of possibilities light years beyond the personal ego.

Is this not where Man appears to be stuck?

Nevertheless, Aquarius has one lesson yet to learn. It simply can't keep carrying around this thing called an ego. The weight of its own personal story has become too unwieldy. Your story is your story is your story. How eternally fascinating can it be? How can you possibly keep from comparing your story to others? Eventually it runs out of steam. Aquarius is ultimately insatiable and must be transcended. This eleventh sign of the "perfected, complete Man" is yet "incomplete." It has to go somewhere . . . but where? It already has everything and is not dependent on others. It has achieved all of its goals. What else can it do?

All that remains is total surrender of the self. Not oblivion but surrender to a higher power: God's will and the sign of Pisces.

Pisces. In this final stage, the entity/non-entity has to let go of the dream that Aquarius has accomplished. Remember that back in the sign of Aries, we saw how God imagined what it would be like to be separate, solely to experience Itself? The dream-illusion of separation began then and it's apropos that the dream comes to an end in Pisces, which is known for being foggy and dreamlike.

When there is no self, there is no separation.

For most of us, this is flat out confusing. Jesus was not lost in the illusion that He was separate. He kept telling ears that could hear that the Father was the One who mattered. "It's not Me, it's My Father!" What He meant was that yes, He stood before you but He added, "I and My Father are One." This is no mere sing-song liturgical phrase. He was talking directly about being a self but at the same time being translucent to the larger Self (God the Father).

No wonder it's so hard for those with heavy doses of the Piscean archetype to survive this consensus world of harsh differences and separation; they're simply not constructed for it. Pisces had to let go of the Aquarian blueprint simply because *it wasn't real* at its truest essence. This is why we hear so much of Pisces being evasive, vague, escapist, non-ambitious and just floating through life. It wants to transcend self-ness, which it can't! What a dilemma in which it finds itself. The last thing Pisces needs is more individuality!

Paradoxically, the thing they desperately need on the material plane is more individuality. So many Pisceans struggle through life because of their lack of a sense of self. They have to get themselves into proper perspective. It becomes about having a self, but not being *of* it. If Pisces cannot handle the "worldly" reality, they have no chance of conquering the other-worldly. It takes a strong ego in order to transcend itself. That is precisely what Jesus, The Buddha, Muhammad, Lao Tzu and other ascended masters have done. So we see once again that casting aside the sign before us without true understanding of what is happening can be foolhardy.

Pisces does need a sense of self but needs to keep it all in balance. That's what Jesus meant when He said, "Of Myself, I do nothing; All things are done through the Father." Since it's been a dream all along anyway, the dream must be relinquished. We've simply forgotten our true nature. "Being One" is no simple matter. Since the evolving being has become full and now is emptied, the mission of the zodiac is complete.

The Three Modes and Four Elements

The Three Modes

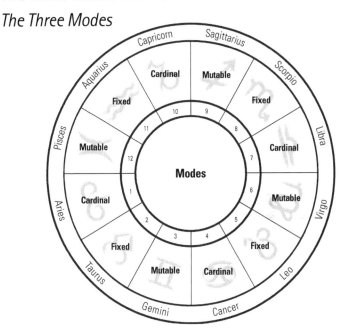

In astrology the modes are basic energies that have been intuited and ascribed to the zodiac from ancient times. All signs fall into one of these three modes: cardinal, fixed or mutable.

Briefly stated, **cardinal** signs are generally leaders and have an innate ability to *generate energy*. The cardinal cross consists of Aries, Cancer, Libra and Capricorn. This does not mean that everyone born to that mode is a leader but, in general, cardinal signs lean towards giving direction, instead of following others. Unless other factors in the chart greatly suppress this type of energy, cardinal people naturally make things happen. They simply have what it takes.

The **fixed** cross consists of Taurus, Leo, Scorpio and Aquarius. These energies are concentrated, focused and organized. Fixed signs *give depth and meaning* to whatever element they represent. Known for being stubborn, these signs plant themselves deeply into whatever they are into and burrow for deeper meaning. You'll find them to be great organizers and researchers. They show much patience and diligence when completing a task. One of the great strengths of this mode is their persistence. They are difficult, if not impossible, to discourage.

The final group of signs, Gemini, Virgo, Sagittarius and Pisces, belong to the **mutable** cross. This energy needs to *disperse and share* each of their respective elements. It is important that mutables distribute to others. Not necessarily adept at generating or finishing a task, this is the most adaptable and flexible of the three modes.

From the perspective of the three modes, the twelve signs look like this:

Aries – cardinal. What better way to "start" the zodiac than with a cardinal sign! Aries gets things going. Known as the pioneer of the zodiac, the Aries archetype is not one to wait around for anything or anyone. Perhaps this is why they are labeled as headstrong. The Ram has a natural tendency to "ram" ahead, push on and inject its personality directly into the immediate environment—sometimes to the dismay of others. They go from point A to point B, period. Everyone else, get out of the way or hurry up!

Taurus – fixed. The second sign needs to affix itself to the earth and become firmly grounded. Life cannot be all fireworks (Aries); therefore, the need to anchor the archetype into something solid and seemingly permanent. If the growing "self" doesn't set down roots now, the stability of the following signs will be shaky. Taureans are great at jobs requiring slow, patient steadiness. They're the tortoise of the zodiac.

Gemini – mutable. The nature of the next archetype is to explore, gather information and disseminate it. Gemini is all about spreading the news. Gemini discovers so much in this symbolic stage of the butterfly; it is the mobile library of the zodiac. They tend to live in the future somewhat because of this, always excited about what's coming next. The reason that they are known for being so changeable is because they constantly react to fluctuating stimuli in their immediate environment. They find *everything* "interesting" and want to tell *everyone* about it.

Cancer – cardinal. We are back to the cardinal mode once again. With the scattering of the seeds of knowledge given us by the Geminian messenger, the need is to start off anew in a fresh direction, one of development. The self has its essence from Aries, its "stuff" from Taurus and can now communicate because of Gemini. In this stage, the celestial embryo is cradled and nurtured in the womb of Cancer the Mother. She leads and defends the pack. Try sticking your finger in the hole where the young crabs are growing and you're gonna get bit!

Leo – fixed. We see now that the symbolic "babe has hatched" in the previous stage, and Leo proceeds to strengthen the expression of that new birth. This "developmental stage" goes on to gain courage and confidence as it learns to grow and compete amongst the other animals of the jungle.

Virgo – mutable. Born anew in Cancer and Leo, Virgo takes over to perfect and assimilate what it has grown to be. The Virgo archetype has an innate need to help others, to share its new abilities. Virgo is here to serve all and rise above Leo's need to be so focused upon itself. Virgo folks are very flexible and usually their ego is so unobtrusive that they'll volunteer for just about any job that needs to be done. Virgo is a humble sign.

Libra – cardinal. The third cardinal sign, Libra, takes the lead once again but this time in a *social* way. This archetype has a natural ability to think on its feet and is ever ready to share ideas with others. It takes the perfected stage of the human from Virgo and debuts it out into the world, which is a big step. Libra is a leader and savvy about the ways of the world.

Scorpio – fixed. Relationships have been established in Libra; now Scorpio ups the ante. The bar is raised now to include the desire, intensity and obsession united through love. Passions escalate as Scorpio focuses heavily on the ramifications of the relationship and the combined value of the pairing. The total is greater than the sum of its parts.

Sagittarius – mutable. Now that deep one-to-one emotions have been established, the need is to broaden our experience and share that new world with all. Sag now showers its good will on all people, knowing little about restriction and limits. Spreading encouragement and enthusiasm (mutable) makes Sag a natural cheerleader of this team.

Capricorn - cardinal. Our final cardinal sign, Capricorn leads by exemplifying the proper ways of acting for the good of all. Self-sacrificing and self-effacing, Capricorn has a strong innate sense of duty, responsibility and stewardship. Being the zodiac's final cardinal sign, the Goat leads us all to the Promised Land. The Moses archetype was of the Capricornian archetype, if any.

Aquarius – fixed. Our final fixed sign takes its position very seriously, concentrating on its place as a member of the global community. Following Capricorn, high-minded Aquarius goes one step farther: its ideals are unparalleled as it concentrates (fixed) on those things that we can all accomplish as a whole. Concentrating on higher thoughts and ideals, the Water Bearer appreciates that utopia does not have to remain just a dream; indeed, it lies within our reach.

Pisces – mutable. The final of the mutable signs, Pisces has an inherent need to spread love throughout the world. Foreign to discrimination, the Fish shares the universal waters with all, seeing no differences between anyone or any group. There's more than enough for all. The zodiac has evolved, once again displaying its exquisite design. The finale is simple: to give love unconditionally.

The Four Elements

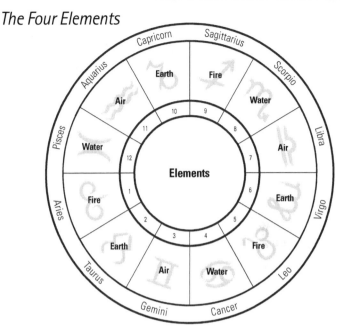

Fire is the first element. Aries, Leo and Sagittarius are full of zest, enthusiasm and spirit. Fire people are usually quite impatient and always itching to get going. They have a strong sense of self and don't easily back down from those with differing opinions. This element is hungry to experience life.

The second group, Taurus, Virgo and Capricorn, make up the **earth** element. They are down-to-earth and practical. Just as their name implies, these are the three that stay close to Mother Earth. Usually, they must be productive to satisfy their archetype. Not always the most emotional, earth signs usually are the first people whom others call upon for practical help of any kind because, in general they are the most dependable of all the signs.

The third element, **air**, is comprised of the signs that are focused on mentality, the mind and ideas. Represented by Gemini, Libra and Aquarius, these are our thinkers. Air signs love dialogue of any kind. The sky is the limit with these cerebral types. Not always practical, many of them live in their minds, in the realm of ideas and possibilities.

Finally, the fourth element, **water**, Cancer, Scorpio and Pisces are primarily based on emotion. These three signs essentially concentrate on their feelings, moods and sensibilities. Water signs differ greatly from the others because emotion is their primary domain. How do they feel? Are they loved? Are they acting in a loving manner? Do they belong?

Dividing the zodiac into these four elements illustrates how different and how similar we all are in terms of our basic motivations and needs. Each sign's natural essence fills them with their particular urge:

Aries – fire. Aries is the essence of fire: active, dynamic, adventurous, uni-directional. They are the pioneers of the zodiac. "Please move aside, I don't mean to run over anyone, I just have to move on! Since I'm the first sign, let's get things started!"

Taurus – earth. Taurus is the essence of earth: grounded, patient, tough, firm. "I'm staying put. I'm digging in for the long haul. You're not budging me! I'm not going to be blown around willy-nilly. I love this place too much and I'm staking my claim."

Gemini – air. Gemini is the essence of air: talking, exploring, curious, playful, communicative. "I have places to discover and many rocks to overturn. Think of all the wonderful things there are in this world. I have so much to see and I can't wait to tell everyone all about it!"

Cancer – water. Cancer is the essence of water: moody, emotional, loving, motherly. "I need my family to stay close by. I feel everything and must watch out that the world does not hurt me. I need a cozy nest where I am safe, and I just love children."

Leo – fire. "I consistently need to express my liveliness! I am colorful and need to spread my peacock feathers so everyone can see my beauty! No, I will not sit down or cut my hair. Life is to be enjoyed!"

Virgo – earth. "Don't call me lazy! I have to work so hard because there's so much to do. Someone has to do it! I don't mind. I get a great feeling from completing tasks. I care enough to go the extra mile and I like helping people."

Libra – air. "I want to know what's going on. I need to be up on the latest trends. Where's my partner so I can bounce some ideas off of him? I must have bright people around me. Life is so fascinating and I want to use my intelligence to play a big role in it."

Scorpio – water. "I am intensely emotional. I don't have time for weakness. I want to devour life. The intensity of life appeals to me and I need a partner with whom to share it. I *know* how you feel, so don't try to hide it from me. Life is all about passion!"

Sagittarius – fire. "I want to have some fun! Doesn't everyone? There are just so many places where one can get bogged down but I want to play! Life has so much enjoyment to offer; I don't want to miss a minute of it. Let's go!"

Capricorn – earth. "Now, let's be sensible. There's a lot to do and it has to be accomplished the proper way. I am willing to sacrifice my needs because I feel a duty to my society. Someone has to be responsible!"

Aquarius – air. "I am so fascinated by all the possibilities of what our minds can do together. Think of it! We don't have to keep doing things the same way. Let's think outside of the box and come up with new ways to address our old problems. If we work together, we could have an ideal world!"

Pisces – water. "All you need is love, and that's the truth. If we love each other, we'll all get by. If we remain sensitive to each other's needs, no one will be left out. Isn't this how it should be?"

Combining the Modes and Elements

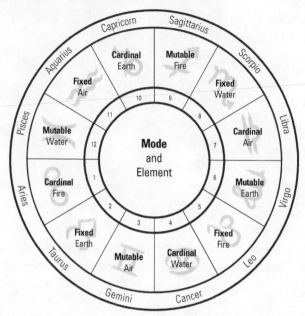

When the modes and elements are combined, we clearly see the individuation that results from this merging into *twelve unique pairings*. It becomes obvious that these combinations describe many of the similarities and differences among each sign. There are twelve and *only* twelve signs to the zodiac: three modes x four elements = twelve signs.

These unique combinations largely define the basic nature of each sign.

Aries – cardinal/fire. The first cardinal sign bursts forth with fire, spirit and enthusiasm. The spark of life has given rise to the first sign of the zodiac. It is unfettered because it *must* be. This is no time to be careful; it's time to GO! This is why those strong with Arian influences in their chart have little patience for obstacles or slow pokes. The fire element is what gives Aries great excitement for life's adventures. It's the combination of cardinal and fire that gives them their essential thrust forward.

Taurus – fixed/earth. Have you ever tried to persuade a Taurean personality? The spark that originated in Aries must now be fixed or anchored. The Taurean urge is to affix itself within a frame of reference; it's here to stay and now needs a connection to something larger in order to sustain itself. They're not simply being stubborn; they're doing their job. Persistence is the middle name of this archetype. What else are they supposed to do, allow Aries to just fly along endlessly until they burn out in space? Because of Taurus, we now have a strong, immovable, solid foundation upon which to build and grow. Many Taureans are very comfortable when they're out digging in their garden.

Gemini – mutable/air. In the previous anchored position of Taurus, things were growing stale. The impulse now is to travel about and see what lies beyond the fortress walls. Gemini is absolutely fascinated with the world around it. It needs to endlessly explore all of the fascinating novelties in its environment and spread stories about its findings. The restless need of mutable/air is to inform everyone of the latest news.

Cancer – cardinal/water. This time the cardinal archetype leads, but with feelings first. "Are you feeling okay?" This is the nursery where the babies get to be watched and cared for. As with all cardinal signs, things start anew. In this stage, the heart is developed as awareness of others emerges. It takes time to adjust to the element of water. Cancers lead by developing and protecting feelings—theirs and others'.

Leo – fixed/fire. The burst of fire (life energy) shored up by fixed traits gives Leo a powerful new confidence in itself. Leo takes the newly born offspring out for a test drive. "This is MY stomping ground; I back down to no one!" Careful construction of our new *feeling* state in Cancer leads to the need to broadcast our newfound self-reliance to the world (actually to the self). Leo's fire is consistent, just like their inextinguishable flame.

Virgo – mutable/earth. Taking over from Leo, Virgo no longer feels a need to crow about its accomplishments or even be noticed. The archetype of the Virgin represents purity of purpose and simply wishes to share its ability to "get the job done." Mutable earth really means serving others so we all can survive this terrestrial challenge. Mutable signs want to help by using the element in which they are steeped. Virgo appreciates the new burst of life given to us by Leo's fire. Now, the blacksmith forges his iron in the hot coals.

Libra – cardinal/air. Again a cardinal sign, again a huge leap forward. Now, we are ready for the world of other people. Libra leads now with ideas (air). Many, many of our famous authors and actors find themselves born to this archetype. With the newly perfected self (Virgo), Libra is compelled to keep up with the "latest" of what's happening socially. The archetype of the Scales builds itself upon the perfection and readiness that has taken place in Virgo. Libra influences our thinking and also teaches us how to think for ourselves.

Scorpio – fixed/water. Scorpio takes the relationship that was born in previous Libra and gives it much more depth and meaning (fixed). This archetypal stage ultimately represents courage. Dedication is everything to Scorpio. Now is the time for more thorough merging. This is why people think of sex and passion when they think of Scorpio. "Fixed water" means concentrated feelings; and that means intense likes and dislikes, which Scorpios are known for.

Sagittarius – mutable/fire. Fireworks all around! The compacted passion that intensifies in Scorpio gives rise to Sag wanting to let loose and spread its pyrotechnics across the sky. Again, following a fixed sign, this mutable archetype wants to share what has just been concentrated. Sagittarius wants to disperse its newly found value of personal closeness (Scorpio) with all. Everybody, come to Disney World and have fun! Mutable fire is all about spreading and sharing enthusiasm.

Capricorn – cardinal/earth. Now that we start into our final cardinal sign, we see that its purpose is one of leading mankind. It's no wonder that this archetype is imbued with a great sense of duty and responsibility. This is the final cardinal sign, and being earthbound, Capricorn wants to do things "the proper way." It is the leader of the zodiac in conceiving and building institutions that are designed to serve and govern us all. Based upon the new idealistic aspirations that Sagittarius dreamt into being, Capricorn has the charge of constructing and maintaining a world built upon those philosophical tenets.

Aquarius – fixed/air. The Water Bearer now finds itself obsessed with organizing all the world's ideas into one workable, coherent mental matrix. This is the seed-sign of the "ramifications of concepts." If *this* is true and *that* is true then think of the possibilities! Clearly the most idealistic and inventive of the dozen, Aquarius gives great mental focus to all that it envisions. Having transcended personal relationships, this air archetype is chiefly intrigued with *how we think as a collective.*

Pisces – mutable/water. Once again, showing the sparkle of the twelve-faceted jewel that is the beautiful ring of the zodiac, we see how Pisces is instilled with the universal urge to give unconditional love to all. Mutable water = *give love.* Aquarius has given us a world where we treat each other as brothers and sisters; now Pisces feels compelled to nurture, accept and include all that lives herein with no exceptions. It is no coincidence that the *exquisite zodiac* concludes with the final sign based upon giving unconditional love. It was building to this pinnacle all along:

> ...*twelve unique pairs of modes and elements.*
> ...*twelve unique archetypes.*

Self-Oriented Versus Other-Oriented Signs

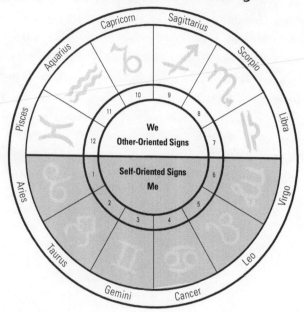

The first six signs of the zodiac are "self-oriented" while the last six are "other-oriented." This by no means implies that the first six signs, Aries through Virgo are all wrapped up within themselves; nor does it mean that the final six signs, Libra through Pisces, are completely absorbed with others. These terms are broad generalities that describe the archetypal impulses that lie at the bases of the lower and upper halves of the zodiac. As you follow along, you will see that the lower half of the zodiac, the self-oriented, is generally about "me and mine"; the top half is about "we and ours."

We must have a strong sense of self in order to even begin to cope with others. This is what is accomplished in the first half:

The self is put together.

The success that occurs during the "we" half is largely dependent upon how well the self develops during the first half. Conversely, if the "developing self" (in the first half) is not exercised and tested, then the self fails to thrive. Either way, both halves are critically important and interdependent.

Keep in mind that most personal natal charts have a mixture of many compatible and competing themes. For instance, a person may have seven planets in self-oriented signs, while another may have just two planets in other-oriented signs. We're each a complex soup of many ingredients.

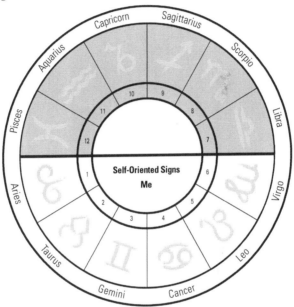

Aries. No sign is as self-oriented as this primary sign. It has to be that way. Many non-Arians marvel at Aries' ability to simply do and say what they feel with little or no regard to other people's thoughts or feelings. This is not because Aries types intend to step on anybody's toes. It's simply because in their world, *they just cannot afford to, or are unable to think of, limitations and obstacles.* They must move ahead; the light is green! "I see something and I head directly towards what I want."

It's that simple.

There *has* to be one sign that is uncomplicated, and that sign is Aries. Certainly, it can go to great extremes and become really irritating to all involved if the Arian personality is too self-focused. Balance is needed in the remaining signs and houses of the birth chart in order to give it more well-roundedness.

Taurus. In a similar fashion, the second sign is also very self-oriented. The Bull is quite satisfied mulling over what they *have*. That is Taurus: me and my stuff. Remember, Taurus digs in and secures itself to the earth, their home and their immediate surroundings. No sign lives in a simpler world yet is completely content. The self-absorbed domain of Aries has blossomed into its immediate surroundings. Taurus appreciates what it has and shows little interest in things beyond its reach. If they don't "own" it, of what use is it? The visceral reaction of this sign is to *enjoy* what they have, and Taurus knows better than anyone how to enjoy the fruits of life.

Gemini. Now, the mind gets involved! The Twins expand their circle as widely as possible. To them, one thing is as interesting as the next, and all is intellectual fodder. "Look at this! Oooh, look at that!" Everything is captivating to this childlike archetype. They are focused and fascinated with how their own mind works.

Now that we are halfway through the self-oriented signs, we see that the symbolically evolving being has a self (Aries), its stuff (Taurus) and its mind and ability to communicate (Gemini). Because of Gemini, our world has been growing broader and more enchanting; now, we can communicate with each other. These basic human attributes should not be taken for granted.

Cancer. Things are becoming more complicated now. Feelings have been introduced to the growing entity, and with feelings comes a sense of vulnerability. Ever ready to crawl under a nearby rock (the family unit) for safety, Cancer is alert to its heart and pines for emotional security. Cancer is very self-oriented, too, but things start to change now. The sense of self-protection is at odds with their new and crucial mothering instinct.

This is a critical cardinal sign and the reason why is simple: Cancer needs to raise their offspring but it doesn't want their loved ones to leave the nest; therefore, a conflict ensues. No sign has more difficulty letting go. They have such a need for their young to stay home because it also makes *them*, the Cancer, feel safe and protected.

The tendency towards codependency is very prevalent here.

Love can be quite conditional here. This archetypal stage is not quite ready for relationships; more development is needed in the last two self-oriented signs, Leo and Virgo, before the evolving self is truly ready to intermix with others. An evolved and balanced implementation of the Cancer principle will love, nurture *and then let go.*

The evolving self benefits greatly from this stage. On the verge of running dry after the first three long travails, the self is finally wetted with the waters of love from its surroundings. The zodiac's inherent intelligence has an impeccable sense of timing.

Leo. Ruled by the Sun, self-oriented Leo is tempted to become too self-involved, partly because fire signs are naturally aligned with "self-focus." In this stage, Leos test the limits of their own confidence. Afforded a stronger sense of self given to them by Cancer, Leos roar across the jungle, heralding their new self-assurance. This new boldness is required before the evolving self is ready to meet others in the first other-oriented sign of Libra.

The Lion grants advancing Man the ability to not quiver in self-doubt and to live in the world unthreatened. Just like a teenager, it is quite natural for Leo to strut its bravado before it can settle back into a healthy sense of dignity. This is a critical stage of development.

If anything, Leo needs to err on the side of cockiness.
Upcoming Virgo will take care of humility.

The extroversion that takes place now is of paramount significance. Thanks to Leo, Cosmic Man stands up tall and ready for the rigors headed its way.

Virgo. We reach the last of the self-oriented signs in Virgo. All must be perfected now and excuses will no longer be tolerated. Virgo senses that

Libra is coming, and along with it comes society. So, what are you to do? Shine your shoes, press your pants, get a haircut and basically get your act together.

Virgo is still self-oriented but that is quickly giving way to a sense of wonder and intrigue over mixing socially. *Virgo puts it all together.* The Virgin is very concerned with any possible impurity that it may have let slip. This is why Chiron fits so well as the ruler of Virgo: cleaning up one's act and purifying the self so that it may start anew in the upper half of the zodiac. Virgo fine-tunes all that has happened so far in the self-oriented half. Virgo's newly born humility bridges the gap perfectly from weighty self-orientation towards mixing with others.

The individual self has swollen to its maximum size in the archetype of Leo and now the Virgin puts the self into perspective. It simply cannot progress any further until it includes the rest of the tribe. Blending with others is basically done to expand the self.

Due to Virgo's hard, honest work, the evolving self is now ready to try on someone else.

Generally speaking, astrology's first six signs see themselves in everyone else,
while the latter six see everyone in themselves.

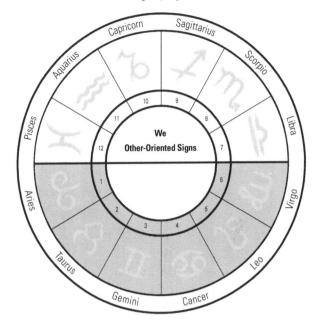

Libra. The critical leap has now been made not only into the next cardinal sign but into the "we" half of the zodiac, the other-oriented signs. Libra clearly is the Aries of the second half of the zodiac. No sign is more obsessed with others than Libra. That's why we have the symbol of the Scales. We have just been "prepared" by Virgo; now we must *compare* ourselves to others in order to get a relative perspective on our new social self. Even though Libra is essentially partner-oriented, it's still quite self-oriented. How can it be otherwise? They are acutely aware of what is going on socially because that is their new domain. What goes on outwardly reflects how they feel inwardly. Because of this compulsive need to feel accepted by society, Libra must be ever vigilant about falling prey to class-oriented thinking.

Clearly, one of Libra's biggest downfalls is also their strength. They are great appeasers and compromisers. This is why they often do well as mediators. On the other hand (Libra's favorite phrase), they sometimes must take a position of their own. It's just the nature of the Scales to tip to one side then back to the other seeking equilibrium.

Keep in mind that Libra is a very smart sign. This is the stage where the self has become self-assured enough to work with another. This archetype is strong in its ability to partner. Because of Libra, we have broken the ice of social behavior. A great step has indeed been taken.

Scorpio. Now we're really getting into it. Talk about other-oriented: Scorpio is emotionally quite obsessed with the other. Theirs is a fierce need to merge and create a sum much greater than the total of the parts. This is truly the stage where life's great ups and downs are encountered. Forget about anything having to do with *surface* behavior. Never mind what others think or how one fits into society in this eighth stage, unless additional planets in the chart are found in Libra.

Scorpio is all about depth, courage and devotion to one another. Once again we encounter the need to value what one has but now it's because two people have truly married and become one. If the relationship does not reflect a bona fide exchange between the couple, then the tendency for an unbalanced relationship is very high. One person may be usurping the other's life energies. These shadowy types will keep you guessing.

This is where the zodiac smolders: the pressure-cooker. Alchemy has occurred. The beauty, strength and character of Scorpio give Cosmic Man purpose and valor. Other-orientation means just that; merging with the other becomes everything here.

Sagittarius. Other-orientation is the perfect category for this sign. Due to the great emotional compression that was just experienced in Scorpio, Sag bursts out into a huge new world of experience. The bigger the better!

Sagittarius is limitless, or so it thinks. Having transcended personal relationships in the previous signs of Libra and Scorpio, Sagittarius invites *everyone* to the party! This stage is so broad, ruling things like philosophy, higher education, government, religion, exchange students and politics. Sag has a feverish desire to travel the planet and see all that there is. Expansion is their middle name and this other-oriented sign is all about sharing its newly burgeoning self with the global community.

This is why they love to read and are usually quite political and soap-boxy. They want to influence the ideas that are governing mankind. Keep in mind that Sagittarius "knows" that Capricorn is coming next, as it approaches the top of the zodiac where the Goat is about to be enthroned.

Because of this fearless Archer, the growing self is expanding to great heights and is energized by its new camaraderie and vistas. Now, being other-oriented includes the masses: the greater collective.

Capricorn. From now on the rest of the signs of the zodiac are becoming more and more other-oriented. Capricorn adds a great sense of duty and responsibility to the maturing zodiac. Not only is it quite aware of others, the evolving being has now become quite stable within itself and senses a need to build a community of laws, structures and institutions in order to have society work as effectively as a well-oiled machine.

Many times the Capricorn actually suffers greatly because they have gone too far: doing everything for everyone else. Self-effacement can get out of hand with this sign because of their "fatherly" need to sacrifice the self for the well being of the whole. The final cardinal archetype, Capricorn is acutely aware of its privileged position atop the zodiac. No sign has a greater sense of obligation to others.

Thank goodness for Capricorn, which paves the way for the final two signs. Now the advancing self has reached the zenith of the zodiac and reigns over the wheel of life with an appropriate sense of responsibility and veneration.

Aquarius. The Water Bearer transcends Capricorn and regains its sense of individual rights. This archetype is truly dedicated to the success of the planet as a whole, making it the most idealistic of the bunch. Other-oriented Aquarius considers others to be just like themselves; that is, equals. Usually very non-judgmental, this eleventh sign is a strong advocate for liberation and universal causes. Concern for the environment is frequently very near the top of their list of priorities.

Because Aquarius has such a great, renewed sense of personal freedom, some do have to watch out for an unbalanced sense of entitlement. Yes, famous figures John Belushi, Yoko Ono, John McEnroe and Betty Freidan were born to this sign; however, I'm not sure how well they knew they were also exemplifying the shadow side of Aquarius. There's a fine line between being disruptive versus liberated for this free-spirited archetype.

Aquarius has become so other-oriented that oftentimes they go by unnoticed. It is one of the most underrated signs of the zodiac. Aquarius has a great sense of tolerance and benevolence. They naturally understand that to help others helps themselves in return . . . enlightened self-interest.

Because of the Water Bearer, who gives back to the rich and vital world, we are all better off from their considerable contributions and generosity. Still, there is a bit of ego that remains in Cosmic Man, a final grain to be cooked.

Pisces. At last, Pisces . . . not because they are the least but because they are the ultimate. By no means does this imply that they are better than any other sign (that is never the case). It is so because Pisces is charged with removing the last impediment to the "individual's" ultimate freedom and enlightenment. Pisces is almost totally other-oriented, many times to a fault.

The *modus operandi* of this final sign is to give to all and bring us all together into one undifferentiated universal family. Having little sense of self is their beauty, as well as their pitfall.

Pisces is here to go beyond the ego (Aquarius) but keep the self in perspective, as did Jesus Christ. Cosmic Man now realizes the futility of serving the self. The preceding eleven signs have managed to satisfy themselves in one way or another but at this pinnacle of signs, the way is paved for total enlightenment.

Yes, at the archetypal level, Pisces masters the sense of being other-oriented. Because Pisces has cleared out the clutter and burden of self-hood, the greater Self can return home to its natural state of Oneness.

Six Polarities of Signs

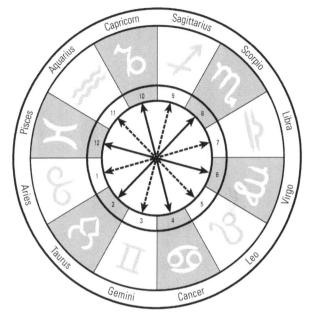

Even a brief discussion of the zodiac's six polarities reveals much about interrelationships in the zodiac. All polarities are made up of two signs that belong to the same mode; that is, cardinal, fixed or mutable. Each sign has its opposite sign. In astrology, it is uncanny how much those two signs are alike even in their differences. It is important to understand these polarities as their themes keep reoccurring throughout translations of natal charts, understanding transits, chart comparisons and many other typical functions in the practice of astrology.

Aries-Libra: Aries begins the zodiac. Much has been written about the archetype of Aries and its focus upon the self. Directly across the zodiac lies the sign of Libra, the first of the other-oriented signs. Aries, so wrapped up in "me," gives rise to Libra, the sign dedicated to partnership, or "we." Aries: "I am"; Libra: "We are."

The grander Self can only learn so much by being self-focused. Once we come "out of ourselves" we paradoxically learn more about ourselves; therefore, Libra essentially does not further itself until it partners with others. A great example of this partnership was John Lennon (Libra Sun sign) and his Gemini song-writing partner, Paul McCartney. Even though they didn't always get along, look what their partnership produced!

This Aries-Libra axis has much to do with the formation of one's identity. You will notice as with all six polarities that the problem one has finds its solution in the sign directly opposite. When Aries becomes too selfish, it needs to activate the Libra side of itself. Libra has a magnificent sense of tact, diplomacy and compromise. On the other hand, because of their strong need for a sounding board, Librans often lose themselves within their partner. When that happens, their antidote is to develop their own Aries side: more self!

Note the comparative values of this axis: Aries/Libra; self/other; me/us, how I look/how we look; my accomplishments/our accomplishments; my identity/our identity; my adventure/our adventures.

Taurus-Scorpio: Taurus is very much embedded within its own self, secure within. Many times we hear of Taurus being the sign of money, collections, valuables, assets. When we look deeper, we see that it represents our sense of *self*-worth. We find ourselves and our value via the archetype of Taurus. This archetype is rough and tough and deeply rooted. Its opposite sign, Scorpio, finds more value or self-worth via wedding itself to *another*. Taurus: my stuff; Scorpio: our stuff. Again, the self can only go so far by itself. More development occurs when we exercise the same trait by sharing it with another, as is done with the steadfast sign of Scorpio.

Taurus sometimes finds itself in self-imposed claustrophobia; that's when it needs another person to share. On the other hand, when Scorpio gets clogged with too much emotional drama in their partnership, their answer lies in simply dealing with their own stuff. We all have all twelve parts within; it's just that most of the time we get too myopically focused on parts of our own dominant impulses.

Scorpio can become obsessed with merging with the other. As was said earlier, no sign can become more enmeshed when it comes to partnerships than Scorpio (and Libra). Scorpio invests much of its own self-worth in the duo. What happens when we base our own self-worth upon another? It can be a shaky proposition.

The Taurus-Scorpio axis can be tempted toward possessiveness or even jealousy. It's like looking down at a game board with moving pieces. When one crosses over the second sign of Taurus to the eighth sign of Scorpio, things get thick. The desire to make things "mine" can get very gooey. Many Taurus and Scorpio personalities can get lost in a sense of "owning" the partner. This rarely works out for those involved. Individuality must not only be preserved but realistic expectations must be developed toward others in order for the union to be healthy.

Any and every soul traversing the zodiac needs to stand tall by itself at some point. You can whistle past Pluto only so many times.

Note the comparative values of this axis: Taurus/Scorpio; my stuff/our stuff; my worth/our worth; my money/other people's money; my little nest/our little nest; I ground myself/I ground myself through you; my stubbornness/our stability.

Gemini-Sagittarius: Things get much lighter now. Gemini: "my mind"; Sagittarius: "our minds."

The Gemini prototype endlessly gathers the new information that eventually leads to its polar opposite, where the collective mind works itself into an overall philosophy. We've discussed Gemini's mercurial need to avoid taking a position or stance. Nothing could be further from the truth than with the archetype of Sagittarius. They'll take a position on anything and everything (think of Ann Coulter). Known as the soapbox sign, Sag has a burning need to stand up for what it believes is truth and let you know about it. What opposites!

Gemini informs the individual mind while the Archer schools itself, travels and forms thought at a higher level. When Gemini has difficulty taking a stance, it needs to borrow a philosophical basis from its Sag counterpart. In reverse, Sagittarius sometimes comes off preachy and ill prepared for argument. It can gain much by drawing upon its Gemini side where more data is available.

Needless to say, this whole mutable axis is much lighter, lifting itself out of the deep muck of Taurus-Scorpio. Mutable differences, by their very nature, give us much less trouble than we run into with the cardinal or fixed paradigms. This is why this polarity holds much less stress.

See the Gemini/Sagittarius polarity at work: smaller/bigger; my ideas/ our philosophies; local community/the world at large; elementary or high school/college or university; small publications/the Internet; short trips/long voyages; casual chit-chat/major debate; gossip/propaganda.

Cancer-Capricorn: The next cardinal twosome is the fourth sign, Cancer, with the tenth, the opposing sign of Capricorn. In both signs the expanding self must *establish a position*: Cancer, within the family and Capricorn in the public arena.

When Cancer becomes too insulated within the family cocoon, exteriorization, or borrowing from its Capricorn half, is necessary. In terms of the opposite, many times worldly businessman Capricorn has gotten far removed from its emotional source and needs to refuel and restore from its roots in watery Cancer.

These are the two signs that leave their respective havens cautiously. Perhaps this is because of their new charge of being cardinal once again. Remember, cardinal signs generate or lead. Sequestered Cancer leads us into the stage of development where everything must be done very carefully; they're vulnerable. Conversely, Capricorn shepherds the way onto the public forum, the most visibly *unprotected* stage that there is.

Note the comparative values of this axis: Cancer/Capricorn; my home/ my office; my family/my staff; emotionally cautious/professionally careful; buffered by family/buffered by social position.

Leo-Aquarius: Leo is based on what "I" can do; Aquarius, what "we" can do. Seated within the first half of the zodiac, Leo finds it imperative to be heard. This assists the developing entity as it overcomes Cancerian hypersensitivity. Faith in the self is firmed up as extroversion leads to self-reliance.

When Leo gets too addicted to its own voice, it must remember the group and not be threatened when others garner attention. Aquarius believes in what can be done as a group. When it lacks something, it must draw upon its Leo core, its individuality.

Here we find ourselves in the final polarity consisting of fixed signs. Fixed signs don't like to move. They like things done *their way*. When we sharpen our study of the half-dozen polarities, we see how we gain when we incorporate the nature of the opposing archetype. Leo must not stay in a state of self-insistence; likewise, Aquarius must learn that others just aren't that interested or invested in the success of the group. We're all different.

Note the comparative values of this axis: Leo/Aquarius; my creation/our creation; my offspring/the world's population; self-confidence/team confidence; self-expression/group expression.

What is the glue that holds this whole magical zodiac together? That comes next.

Virgo-Pisces: Again we have two mutable archetypes, and these two signs are usually not "full of themselves" in any way. This is a critical dyad, indeed. Virgo, the archetype of discrimination is like black and white when compared to Pisces, the sign of indiscrimination. Virgo, the sign of exclusion; Pisces, the sign of inclusion.

In almost every case, when Virgo loses perspective it's because they are being too particular. The opposite is true for Pisces. These two energies absolutely must work together in harmony. Cosmic Man needs Virgo to tell us exactly when it's safe to cross the street. On the other hand, Pisces is needed so that those on opposing sides of the street don't start fighting.

Both signs share a great need to serve. Virgo does not seem to be motivated by trans-Saturnian outer planets (universal principles); that is, it does what's right versus what's wrong. To Virgo, the world is all about differences. Pisces, however, seems to do what is "right" because it is *one* with the other. What it does to you, it does to itself. There are no differences to Pisces.

Virgo's need is to fix things; Pisces' intention is to leave them be. Ruled by Chiron, Virgo prides itself in fixing what is "wrong" (the perfectionist). The Pisces way is to leave things alone because they're already *perfect*. However, letting things go out of laziness or apathy is a common Piscean problem. Both Virgo and Pisces are critically needed and it's no coincidence, once again, that the zodiac concludes with Pisces. The end of positionality, Pisces accepts all as being perfect as it is.

Note the comparative values of this axis: Virgo/Pisces; separateness/oneness; non-discrimination/discrimination; exclusive/inclusive; detail-oriented/non-detailed; fixing/allowing; finicky/accepting; hardworking/tendency to relax; realist/non-realistic; practical/dreamy; driven/adaptable.

Each month as we experience lunations—that is, full moons, new moons, lunar eclipses or solar eclipses—we see these very same polarities come into play. For example, when there is a full moon in Cancer, the mood will be hypersensitive because of Cancer's archetype. What we oftentimes fail to realize is that the opposite *pole* is being activated, too! We then are likely to experience a tug of war between home (Cancer) and career (Capricorn).

By way of another example, let's assume that there will be an eclipse in Aries. The other pole will be activated, too, in the sign of Libra. During the period of the eclipse, we'll feel somewhat torn between taking care of me (Aries) and focusing more on our partnerships (Libra).

A solid understanding of the six polarities will add much to your astrological perceptions and knowledge. The bottom line is that the polarities are essentially inseparable.

Ruling Planets of Each Sign

Consensus regarding planetary rulerships of the signs has changed throughout the ages. By and large, the following discourse on rulership reflects modern thought, including a few of my own recommendations.

It is not an easy task to describe exactly what a "ruling planet" is. For instance, Saturn is said to be ruler of Capricorn. While that match-up is vividly clear to anyone who has at least a basic understanding of the archetypes of the *planet* Saturn and the *sign* of Capricorn, one must keep in mind the difference between a planet and a sign. Many Capricornian traits "come from" or are symbolized by the planet Saturn, while other attributes belong exclusively to the sign Capricorn. There are some subtle differences. In time, with more exposure to natal charts, you will start to be able to sense what the archetype of the ruling planet feels like versus the archetype of the sign that it rules.

Aries is ruled by Mars

Astrologers know from plenty of experience that Mars is warlike, direct and aggressive. Ares was the Greek god of war. Mars correlates well with the first self-oriented sign of Aries. Aries generally do not hold back; they fight for their own needs with no strings attached. Mars and Aries do not hesitate to plunge directly into experience. Yes, both can be blunt, self-serving and harsh at times. The combustibility of these two is like an explosion. The "big bang" of the zodiac is quite occupied with exploding unto itself. In the scheme of things, there is no other manifestation going on at this point in time. Life at this stage has yet to become complex. No planet represents the act of initiation more than Mars.

We can see why Mars and Aries, at the archetypal level, are simply not aware of their environment. They are so busy giving birth to the whole zodiacal circle. There is no "other." Aries is charged with coming into being; his hands are full enough as it is, and the rest naturally follows.

Taurus is ruled by the Earth and possibly co-ruled by Venus

Traditional astrology has always paired the planet Venus with Taurus and Libra; however, I have compiled much evidence and experience that have led me to conclude that the sign of Taurus must be ruled *by the Earth itself*. Taurus' great need to be grounded, their desire for simplicity, their patient way of processing life and their love of the earth itself certainly lends toward this assignment.

A friend called me the other day to tell me that her Taurus boyfriend had just built a huge bonfire in their backyard. She said he scratched out an area in the dirt next to the fire and was lying down in it, right next to the roar. "It makes me feel good," he told her. She understood. I laughed and said to myself, "Earth."

That natural inclination is not Venusian in any way.

Much thought and research needs to be given to this subject because the Earth's position in the zodiac is generally not tracked in western astrology. A big adjustment will need to be made in order to consider the Earth as ruler of Taurus, for many reasons beyond the scope of this book. We will need to evaluate this new archetypical pairing. It presents a dramatic alteration with regard to translating the standard birth chart itself. Consider the Earth: grounded, substantial, unrefined, physical, materialistic and rich. It belongs with Taurus.

It is quite likely that Venus will be kept as *co-ruler* of Taurus but only time will tell.

Just as the fires of Aries and Mars continue to burn, the intelligence of the planets anchors us in the Earth in the sign of Taurus—all to prepare us for the upcoming blustery winds of evolution that will come to us via Mercury: Gemini and the mind itself.

Gemini is ruled by Mercury

Mercury, the swift-winged messenger god (the Greek's *Hermes*) matches the sign of Gemini perfectly. The quick mercurial mind of Gemini is ever exploring new topics and vistas. The swift planet Mercury flies closest to the Sun and needs to keep on moving or it will symbolically "burn up." Staleness is the bane of Gemini. They need constant change and new surroundings. It makes sense to see Mercury soar upwards from the stable, grounded influence of the Earth in the previous sign of Taurus.

Cancer is ruled by the Moon

Just like the sign of Cancer, the Moon is extremely moody and is filled with feeling and longing. Probably the most complex (and most irrational) of all the planets, the Moon reflects the light of the Sun. The Moon's light is not its own but is ever dependent on reflecting the Sun's rays; therefore, it's appropriate that Cancers are known for being dependent upon their family unit, especially the mother: its source.

The study of astrology gives us a long list of keywords for the Moon and Cancer: family, home, children, nest, women, emotion, background, lineage, property, upbringing. The lunar part of a birth chart symbolizes our historical and even karmic background. It represents the unconscious and its roots lie deeply buried. Lunar people (those with strong Cancerian traits or significant placements of their Moon) have a greater need to feel loved and emotionally secure. You can talk until you are as green as the man in the Moon but if a Cancer feels unsafe, that basic issue has to be addressed. They need lots of reassurance. These are all lunar qualities.

The Moon is traditionally known as the second most important planet in a chart, even though it and the Sun are not *planets* in the astronomical sense. The Moon represents the feeling side of a human, the right brain. As wisdom points out, the emotion-based right brain will lead us to truth, love and enlightenment, while the best the analytical (left) side can do is describe what is happening in a contextual manner.

The position of the Moon in a chart is extremely important. Just as with the sign of Cancer, the Moon, nestled deeply into our very being, indicates what makes us feel comfortable. In order to understand people with strong amounts of lunar energy, we must realize that rationality is not their forte, while making sure that you feel "okay" is. This is why the archetypes of Cancer and the Moon represent the mothering instinct. It also explains why you might see a couple that doesn't look compatible, only to find that they are very complimentary; in other words, they are comfortable together and have "great chemistry," most likely because their Moon placements are in harmony.

> *Good chemistry means that when two people's charts are compared, they have planets that line up in geometric harmony known as "aspects."*

Do you see how feelings have evolved out of the plethora of ideas that Mercury and Gemini have drummed up? Evolving man is becoming fuller and continues to unfold into a more robust and complete expression.

Leo is ruled by the Sun

Leo's warmth comes from the Sun, the heart and hearth of the zodiac. This exuberant, expressive sign gets its solar flare/flair from our nearest star. As with the Sun, it needs to be center stage or else the world falls apart! This is one reason why Leos feel entitled to that predominant position. Another exemplary trait of this sunny sign is their abhorrence of triteness, bickering, smallness and, in general, lack of dignity. Leos are a very generous, magnanimous group.

You cannot stop the powerful solar rays, nor would you want to. It is *the* very planet of ego (for better or worse), source of creativity and sense of well being, and life itself. What better way to overcome the lunar apprehensions of Cancer than with great pride, fire, power and confidence?

Virgo is ruled by Chiron (Well, not in most books but that's my take on it!)

Traditional astrology has Virgo and Gemini both being ruled by Mercury. To me, there's no doubt about this one: Chiron, the minor planet, rules Virgo. (Like the new classification for Pluto, the minor planet called Chiron is also categorized as a "Centaur." Since its discovery in 1977, many astrologers have given Chiron the respect it deserves now that we have discerned its significance; therefore, astrologers also refer to it as a planet.)

Astronomical bodies reveal their truths to us when we are ready to hear.

Chiron's nature matches perfectly with Virgo and resolves so many of the doubts astrologers have had regarding Mercury's rulership of Virgo. The main reason is that Mercury is neither Earth-like nor perfectionistic.

Chiron, the Centaur, urges us to greatness and it wants no reward. True nobility is his. Now Mercury can relax and just be concerned with Gemini. (That would keep any planet's "hands" full enough.)

It's not so much that Virgos are perfectionistic, it's more the fact that they *care*. This archetype is closely tied with the subject of wounds, and Chiron is known as the "wounded healer." Virgo is very much an underrated sign and that's how they like it. Likewise, its rock-like ruler enjoys its anonymity, too. What does the quiet Virgo hear from the silent influence of Chiron? There is much to learn but it seems to foretell our fate and our *dharma*, if you will. We are pulled in its direction almost as if we have no choice. Epic events happen in our lives when the planet

Chiron is activated in our charts. Chiron is proving to be a major force in astrological charts, much more than previously thought. There are many mysteries about Chiron and many questions remain about this relative newcomer to our zodiac. Only with time will astrologers be able to grasp its fuller nature.

Libra is ruled by Venus

It is clear that Venus, the planet of beauty, rules the alluring sign of Libra. In astrology, Venus' domain is expressions of beauty in all of its forms: physical appearance, music, art, aesthetics and style. Librans can't abide anything done in a crass or indelicate manner. Libra is the zodiac's ballerina. Venus prompts Libra towards tasteful elegance; both are smooth, fluid energies and are always a class act. They ease the troubled waters and gently nudge us towards maintaining harmonious partnerships to compromise and work together.

The much-needed genteel energies that are given to us by Venus and Libra are a welcome relief after the fiery storms of the Sun and Leo and the blood, sweat and tears of Chiron and Virgo.

Scorpio is ruled by Pluto

In the early days, before we could see Pluto, Scorpio and Aries were both ruled by Mars. Since Pluto's discovery in 1930, a perfect match has been made wedding Pluto to Scorpio. Pluto rules the masses, as well as the shadows and secrets of life. It's the domain of the unconscious. From Pluto's icy distant perch, it insists that Scorpio questions each and every motive for purity of intention. This inquisition also extends to all of their partnerships. They don't fool themselves; therefore, they aren't fooled by others.

Nevertheless, no sign has more of a negative reputation or scares more people. Much of this wariness emanates from the planet Pluto, <u>not the sign Scorpio</u>. Granted, much of it is unfair and unwarranted but as we examine closer, we find that two tendencies of Pluto make many people uneasy. In fact, these same two reasons are what separate the "good" Scorpios from the shadowy types.

1. How does the Scorpio handle every one of their motives being scrutinized by Pluto? (Do they become suspicious of others' motivations?)
2. Is there a resulting significant degree of self-loathing?

As we evolve through the zodiac, we now see the great depths that Pluto and Scorpio have added to the sublime partnering of Venus and Libra. The zodiac is getting warmer.

Sagittarius is ruled by Jupiter

The largest of the planets, Jupiter rules the most expansive sign of the zodiac, Sagittarius. The red giant has always been referred to as the "Great Benefic," "the good guy" And "the good luck planet." While known for their devil-may-care, light-hearted attitude, Sagittarians nevertheless pick up great social idealism from Jupiter.

Jupiter has a natural never-say-die, optimistic nature. Sometimes this actually becomes blind-optimism but needless to say, Jupiter/Sagittarius is the upbeat cheerleader of the dozen. Jupiter influences Sag to be explorative, broad, educated and to let things roll off their backs. No worries.

From the intense fires of passionate Pluto and Scorpio we come to find Jupiter and Sagittarius ready to loosen things up and let go. Sag is about fun, enjoyment and spirit. Isn't that why we're here? The zodiac is starting to get the idea.

Capricorn is ruled by Saturn

Sorry, there just isn't a "lite" version of heavy duty Saturn, the planet surrounded by ice rings. Traditionally, Saturn has been known as the planet of fear, limitation, restriction and death. In the Dark Ages of astrology, it was known as the "Great Malefic." Unfairly and unjustly given those ancient curses, Saturn-the-stern did and still does influence Capricorn to take life seriously but its reputation is much less formidable these days. Saturn finally is getting its legitimate reputation in the zodiac.

Saturn is not here to cause us pain. The archetypes of Saturn and Capricorn are here to make sure life gets "done." That's why these two solemn forces are commonly dreaded to the point of paranoia. But, if *they* aren't going to make sure, who or what will? If your teacher or parent didn't insist that you work hard at your homework, how equipped to handle life would you be? That's the pure intention of Saturn.

Saturn is the father symbol of the zodiac and greatly imbues Capricorn with a selfless sense of duty and responsibility. If the job involves sternness, governance or sacrifice . . . well, that's just part of life. This may sound quite parental but Saturn only respects the responsible.

Capricorn and Saturn care about the whole, the community, the world.
It's their job to keep it together.

And that's precisely why Capricorn conforms; it is the first archetype of sacrifice. New Age astrologers appreciate Saturn for the critical role it plays and for the necessary, unappreciated, overlooked value that it brings to the table. If you don't have a strong Saturn in your chart, you are less likely to go far in this world.

Saturn/Capricorn has taken the helm from expansive, fun-loving Jupiter/ Sagittarius. Because of their contributions, the zodiac is now prepared to take on the world in a larger sense, as it hands the jug of life-giving waters over to Aquarius.

Aquarius is ruled by Uranus

In the olden days, Aquarius was ruled by Saturn. As the telescope has revealed more and more about the planets, Aquarius came to be paired with Uranus. The latest thinking, per Richard Tarnas (one of the world's finest astrological minds), however, has it associated with the archetype of Prometheus, the Greek Titan who stole fire from Zeus in order to give it to the mortals (but that is another story for another time.) Uranus, the idiosyncratic planet that rolls through space spinning on its "side," rules innovation, revolution, liberation and is the harbinger of new ages. Uranian energy fits perfectly with the sign of Aquarius. It abhors the status quo and impels us to find novel remedies to outmoded habits.

Uranus/Aquarius tries to figure out the Big Picture. It's the wizard who is way, way ahead of its time.

Uranus influences Aquarians to be themselves, imbuing them with a great sense of individuality. Known for their tolerance for other people, Aquarians are the greatest "friends" of the zodiac. That concept should not be taken lightly, as this archetype brings us higher ideals via the Aquarian mind. Aquarius bestows friendship upon the collective mindset and contributes ever-broadening spiritual norms.

Uranus keeps us progressing and evolving into something new. Some force has to break up the form that Saturn/Capricorn had established, one that eventually grew old and stale and antiquated. That force is Uranus; it regains the true human self that overly conformed and lost itself in the previous sign of Capricorn, and it fills Aquarius with this wonderful, wonder-filled awe that sees the world as one full of endless possibilities.

Pisces is ruled by Neptune

As with all endings, the sign of Pisces brings us full circle. Previously ruled by expansive Jupiter, now we assign Piscean energies to that ethereal god of the sea, Neptune. Pisces lives to give love and its source is truly unbounded and endless. Neptune's subtle but undeniable force gives Pisces an inexpressible sense of universal oneness. Pisceans don't know how to differentiate; all is one big family to the archetype of the Fishes.

Neptune dissipates imaginary, unreal boundaries that man constantly reconstructs in a desire to protect false ego-mirages. It does so in order to bring us back home, back to Heaven. Neptune/Pisces is the ultimate energy/sign of the zodiac not because it is better than any other but precisely because it doesn't want to overshadow anybody. Its nature has to be what it is, one that transcends the illusion of individuality. Pisces is not in any hurry. To the sign of Pisces, there is nowhere to go and nothing needs to be done. (Tell that to its opposing sign of Virgo!) It reigns in a timeless space and intuitively knows that we have never left home to begin with.

Part Four:

Multi-Faceted And Flawless:
The Jewel of the Universe

The zodiac is a reflection of God's exquisite universe.

So there you have it. We have examined six archetypal variants that spell out why the signs are the way they are: the twelve stages of man, how each sign is an outgrowth of the previous sign, the modes and elements, the self-oriented and other-oriented halves of the zodiac, the six polarities and the twelve ruling planets. Certainly, there are more variants that pertain to the differences among the signs but I believe that these six are the most fundamental. If understood properly, they will help you to see how each sign fits perfectly into its specific position. When we factor in the archetypes of the eleven transiting planets, we can easily understand answers to questions such as, "What's gotten into you?" and "Why are you so stubborn/flighty/intense (fill in the blank)?" The archetypal patterns at the basis of astrology are, of course, the basis of all life. Just as diamonds are formed at the earth's mantle, this intelligence and order comes from a place deep, deep within us. These energies represent very intimate yet universal impulses that often guide us without our conscious knowledge.

A thread of divine intelligence weaves its way throughout the zodiac. It knows what it is doing and provides the foundation for all of life, just as a rose knows how to be a rose and a snowflake knows how to have precisely six sides. There are no mistakes. The zodiac has a built-in, self-contained, self-regulating mechanism. It takes care of itself.

When it lacks in vitality, it draws life energy from Aries, Leo and Sag. When it has to think itself out of a tight spot, it draws upon the Gemini-Libra-Aquarius triad. If it gets too dried up and needs to be nurtured, it summons Cancer, Scorpio and Pisces. And finally, when it becomes destabilized, it grounds itself in Taurus, Virgo and Capricorn.

In a word, the zodiac is "flawless." There is an innate wisdom that only God can inform while maintaining perfect harmony. A person who keeps his life in perfect balance (or close to it) doesn't need to consult with an astrologer or to even know their natal chart. They are naturally in sync with their life force, as well as the ebbs and flows of the life's currents. They *listen* to themselves, while most of us don't. We need all twelve archetypes to be interlaced with each other for a complete and balanced inner life. Fortunately, we each have all twelve archetypes within us. It's our life challenge to keep them in balance.

The zodiac is like a house of mirrors that makes total sense.

We now find ourselves consciously within a new quantum holographic universe. We're far from truly understanding what that means, yet somehow, we just know that the truths that underlie the zodiac also underlie all things. Try to omit or add a sign and it just won't work; it's unnatural. Look what happened in January of 2011 when the constellation of Ophiuchus tried to edge its way into the standard zodiac, portraying itself as the "new" thirteenth sign: it didn't have a chance. Many people erroneously thought that the zodiac had shifted and that they had a new "Sun sign." But, in astrological circles, the zodiac reverted back to its natural order of twelve signs. Nature is mathematical and harmonic at its basis; it has no other possible choice. The zodiac has twelve signs, just like the number of notes in the chromatic music scale, people on a jury, months in a year, inches to a foot, items in a dozen and the number of Apostles. There is no difference. Inherent to the twelve signs of the zodiac are all of the truths that have been elucidated throughout this book. There are twelve sides to this exquisite jewel.

If anything, the zodiac teaches that each of us is connected to a much broader, wiser realm of omniscience and ordered existence—and, we *are* all connected. How do I, as an astrologer, know what I know when I *shouldn't?* I read your blueprint, or birth chart; it tells me who you are. There is no simpler way to put it. It's your calendar and your map. It's your personal design, your paradigm, your seed diagram. It's the true you and is totally natural. It represents the moment frozen in time of your own personal Big Bang.

We can only marvel at this brilliant zodiacal diamond and its clear-cut facets with distinct demarcations of one face to the others— twelve unique mirrors and windows comprising one beautiful gem. All of these innumerable permutations exist within one exquisite zodiac, cohesively "mounted" together by its indigenous common denominator: universal love.

Clearly, we have seen that we are expressions of an empyreal, archetypal design. It has many names, theories and myths. As we continue to wonder about our very nature, we cannot help but sense this orderly, intelligent universe. Each of us has our own way of describing it but several things are vivid: we are in a magical incarnation in which much of our existence seems planned and, at the same time, we know that we have the gift of free will. The study of astrology helps us to better understand our place in this phenomenal cosmos.

God's universe has never been nor will ever be in the same state twice. Its glorious and grand design is never to be replicated—just as you, in all of your multi-faceted magnificence, cannot be expressed twice. You are the emissary of the *nature of the moment* in which you were born.

About the Authors

Rick DiClemente is not your typical astrologer. Widely known as a "way shower," he blends math-science and spiritual-psychic ability with empirical knowledge in order to reveal the multi-faceted story in each chart. Rick's intuitive-astrological readings are like a sit-down with a trusted friend who has your ultimate best interests at heart. At the same time, he brings alive the applied discipline of consulting with the cosmos for timeless wisdom that helps others better understand themselves, their relationships and their lives.

Rick has practiced astrology for 35 years, and has presented numerous lectures, classes and workshops. He makes frequent guest appearances at holistic expos and in the media. Formerly, Rick worked as a documentary filmmaker and computer database manager—both of which inform his work today.

To learn more about Rick, visit *www.starself.com*

Liza Jane Brown first began to appreciate the value of celestial guidance as a young girl, when she enjoyed the vegetables her great grandmother grew according to the phases of the Moon. Encouraged and supported in her endeavors by at least three generations of women who have relied upon astrology's truth, Liza has been a student and practitioner of astrology for 36 years so far. She is also a medical social worker.